Black Men in Britain

While extensive attention has been paid to black youth, adult black British men are a notable omission in academic literature. This book is the first attempt to understand one of Britain's hidden populations: the post-*Windrush* generation, who matured within a post-industrial British society that rendered them both invisible and irrelevant. Using ethnography, participant observation, interviews and his own personal experience, and without an ounce of liberal angst, Kenny Monrose pulls no punches and presents the reader with a fierce but sensitive study of a population that has been vilified and ignored.

The widely disseminated portrait of black maleness, which habitually constructs black men as being either violently dangerous, or social failures, is challenged by granting black men in Britain the autonomy to speak on sociologically significant issues candidly and openly for themselves. This reveals how this group has been forced to negotiate a glut of political shifts and socially imposed imperatives, ranging from *Windrush* to Brexit, and how these have had an impact on their life course. This provides a cultural uplift and offers an authenticated examination and privileged insight of black British culture.

This book will be of interest to sociologists, cultural historians and criminologists engaged with citizenship, migration, race, racialisation and criminal justice.

Kenny Monrose is an Affiliated Researcher in the Department of Sociology at the University of Cambridge, and a College Research Associate at Wolfson College, Cambridge.

Routledge Advances in Ethnography

Edited by Dick Hobbs, University of Essex, and Les Back, Goldsmiths, University of London

Ethnography is a celebrated, if contested, research methodology that offers unprecedented access to people's intimate lives, their often-hidden social worlds and the meanings they attach to these. The intensity of ethnographic fieldwork often makes considerable personal and emotional demands on the researcher, while the final product is a vivid human document with personal resonance impossible to recreate by the application of any other social science methodology. This series aims to highlight the best, most innovative ethnographic work available from both new and established scholars.

Black Men in Britain

An Ethnographic Portrait of the
Post-Windrush Generation

Kenny Monrose

Routledge
Taylor & Francis Group

LONDON AND NEW YORK

First published 2020
by Routledge
2 Park Square, Milton Park, Abingdon, Oxon OX14 4RN

and by Routledge
52 Vanderbilt Avenue, New York, NY 10017

Routledge is an imprint of the Taylor & Francis Group, an informa business

British Library Cataloguing-in-Publication Data
A catalogue record for this book is available from the British
Library

Library of Congress Cataloging-in-Publication Data
Names: Monrose, Kenny, author.
Title: Black men in Britain : an ethnographic portrait of the
post-Windrush generation / Kenny Monrose.
Description: First. | New York : Routledge, 2019. |
Series: Routledge advances in ethnography | Includes
bibliographical references and index.
Identifiers: LCCN 2019025376 | ISBN 9780815354307
(hardback) | ISBN 9781351133432 (ebook)
Subjects: LCSH: Men, Black–Great Britain–Attitudes. | Men,
Black–Great Britain–Social conditions. | Middle-aged men–Great
Britain–Attitudes.
Classification: LCC HQ1090.7.G7 M65 2019 | DDC 305.38/
896041–dc23
LC record available at https://lccn.loc.gov/2019025376

ISBN: 978-0-815-35430-7 (hbk)
ISBN: 978-1-351-13343-2 (ebk)

Typeset in Times New Roman
by Swales & Willis, Exeter, Devon, UK

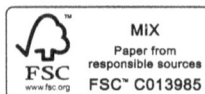

MiX
Paper from
responsible sources
FSC
www.fsc.org   FSC™ C013985

Printed in the United Kingdom
by Henry Ling Limited

This book is dedicated to my dear father Georges Monrose who fell asleep in April 2019. Psalm 121.

Contents

Acknowledgements

Many thanks to the staff at Routledge, especially Emily Briggs, Lakshita Joshi and Elena Chiu. I would like to thank Professor Dick Hobbs, Professor Les Back, Dr Rob Hornsby, Professor Lez Henry, Dr Martin Glynn and Suzanne Hobbs for supporting the intentions of this text. I also would like to thank the late Professor Michael Banton for calling me out at the Mannheim Institute of Criminology at LSE during the very early stages of my PhD. This was an experience that challenged my thinking, and resulted in a friendship involving many long lunches together at the George & Dragon in Downe in Kent. I'd like to say a very special thank you to Dr Monica Moreno Figueroa and the Department of Sociology at Cambridge University for their continued support, as well as the President and staff of Wolfson College Cambridge. I must also thank Tony Russell who, albeit very late in the day, directed me to some essential music to soothe me through the final straight. Charley Patton, Blind Lemon Jefferson and Howlin' Wolf complemented my writing backdrop of Mighty Sparrow, Erik Satie, Joe Higgs and Freddie McKay. Last and by no means least, a huge thank you to all those who afforded me the privilege of spending some incredibly valuable time together. Unfortunately, some have passed away, but their offerings will remain with us, and their insight and light will provide a lamp for our feet.

Chapter 1

Introduction

Personal curiosity and research trajectory

One of the experiences that propelled the challenge of writing this book occurred shortly after I had completed the 'Knowledge of London',[1] and became a licensed (black) London taxi driver. I was twenty-three, raised in a neglected part of East London, and granted a license from the Metropolitan Police to roam the grey streets of London in order to earn an honest wage. This was both an adventurous and an overwhelming experience, as I discovered parts of London that my parents, who had arrived in London from the Eastern Caribbean almost thirty years previously, never had the privilege of seeing.

A cold, wet evening during 'kipper season'[2] found me plying for hire at Euston station. Being 'kipper season', there was not much work on offer, so to pass time I struck up a conversation with another cabbie whom I shared the rank with. Chester, an arresting thickset Barbadian in his late seventies, bragged of being one of London's first black 'black taxi' drivers. As a *Windrush* arrival, he considered himself somewhat of a pioneer, and was full of advice for an inexperienced 'butter boy'[3] like myself. After a long wait and whilst ushering a fare into his cab, in his heavy Barbadian burr he said to me:

> Listen, young man, if you're smart in this country, you can be anybody you want to be, at any time. You can be an African, West Indian or an Englishman. Being a black man in this country is easy, you just have to know what part to play.

Chester drove off and left me to digest not only the acrid diesel smoke from his exhaust, but the potency and clout of his statement. Although I never saw him again, his words planted a seed of inquisitiveness in my mind that lasted many years. How on earth could it be easy to be a black and British? Even as a child, my experience taught me that being black in Britain was problematic. Being black and born in the 'City of Thieves', as Canning Town in Newham was locally known, one learnt early on what you were, who you were and where you belonged. Football grounds, Cub Scout huts and pubs were not for the likes of me. Despite the introduction of racial discrimination law in the

1960s, the colour bar mentioned by Banton (1967) and Sutcliffe and Smith (1974) was still very present when I was growing up during the Thatcherite period.[4] In Newham, this meant many no-go areas for blacks, particularly the south of the borough near to the docks, where I was born.

Blacks throughout London grew accustomed to staying close to where small West Indian communities had emerged and developed into neighbourhoods where they felt safe, and could maintain their own relevant and workable cultural practices. When they did venture from these spaces, it was often for an annual day visit to a provincial seaside town such as Southend-on-Sea, Margate or Clacton. West Indians were fully aware of the significance of the seaside to the English, and despite the host of daily difficulties they encountered, the trip to the seaside was one occasion when they tried their best to shoehorn themselves into British culture.

I recall these trips vividly. Off we went to be English for the day, three, four or five extended black families travelling east towards where the brass bands played the 'tiddly-om-pom-pom' – the fabled British seaside. Fathers and uncles dressed as sharp and dandy as they did upon their arrival on the *Orbita* and *Empire Windrush*.[5] Mothers, sisters and aunties struggled as they carried heavy packed lunches and additional layers of clothing in fear of the sea (Thames Estuary) breeze. We boys were decked out in our best attire, normally reserved for Sunday Mass, and our faces shone with Vaseline. We clung tightly to the two 'bob'[6] we had to spend, and were excited to be doing the same thing that our white classmates did during the six-week summer holidays. We must have been quite a sight, sitting on the shingle, salt marshes and mudflats, eating fish cakes and fried dumplings, arguing about where the sand had gone, and why the sea was brown.

My first experiences of the seaside awakened me to the difficulties associated with my cultural identity, and left me feeling horridly uncomfortable, with a yearning to return to the inner-city enclave. Quickly I realised the subtle implications that the colour bar presented and why our parents rarely ventured away from Newham. I became aware of just how out of context we were. White people pointed, and stared intensely at us. The legion of noisy amusement arcades around us seemed to fall silent and redundant as we passed by – we now were the new object of amusement. Toothless old ladies looked at us open-mouthed, frozen. Old men with handkerchiefs tied on their heads stood in socks and sandals, fixated, whispering loudly about us to each other, while white children our age gesticulated, mocked and looked confused all at the same time. To be honest, it was not malevolent, nor menacing, but eerily strange and disconcerting. Why are they looking at me like that? I eat fish and chips, and drink Tizer. Look, don't you know that I love football? I have posters of Bobby Moore, Kenny Dalglish and Clyde Best on my bedroom wall. Am I not a part of you? Does not I mean we?

Years later, going 'home' to the Caribbean for the first time as an adult, similar issues were raised, only this time in reverse. Almost immediately on exiting the British Airways aircraft, and being thumped by the tropical heat, I was hit by fascinated stares and rapt glances, not only from over-zealous customs employees but from those all around. The difference this time was that these eyes were not grey, blue or green, but big, brown and wide like mine. Again those feelings of being out of context returned. I heard a baggage porter call out, 'Hey, Englishman, let me help you,' and wondered who he was talking to; it couldn't have been me, could it? I had never been called English before (other than by siblings in jest), but it was me. I was finally being called English. I always wanted to be English, but hadn't felt allowed to be, and here I was several thousand miles away from East London, finally being acknowledged as an 'Englishman' (how the St Lucians knew I was English by simply looking at me is something I still marvel at).

Until that moment, I had given up my pursuit of being British, and considered myself a St Lucian. This was of great significance because as the only family member born in England, I was an anomaly at home. This, however, was not a problem, because I became St Lucian by association, and had always referred to it as home (despite not having been there). In time, I learnt how deluded this type of consciousness was. The Eastern Caribbean, like the East End of London, did not acknowledge or accept me culturally, and the same questions from my childhood were again raised. Am I not a part of you?

Waiting for my transportation to arrive in the Windwards' searing heat, I remembered Chester the cabbie, and the exchange we had on that cold wet evening in central London. I recalled the writing of Paul Gilroy, Stuart Hall, Ken Pryce and Michael Banton regarding the difficulties of blackness in Britain, and, submerging myself within their theories, was reminded of the double- and sometimes triple-encrusted consciousness of which they speak. I recalled the fabulous novels I had read by Sam Selvon and George Lamming and the poetry of Sir Derek Walcott, who all reminded me of the heavy burden that manifold identities sometimes carry. Why is it I only feel English in the Caribbean, and a West Indian whilst in Britain? Why do those born in the West Indies arrive in Britain and only then discover themselves as West Indians? Why do blacks born in Britain cleave so much to the Caribbean, whilst those born in the Caribbean cleave to the ideals of 'Britishness'? Why is it so difficult to be a black male in Britain? How does this cultural mishmash of identity have an impact on broader sociological issues? And, most importantly, what does it mean to be a black man in Britain?

The structure of the book

In order to answer these questions, this book examines the life stories and narratives of the post-*Windrush* generation in Britain. The book is a shift away from the habitual analysis of black youth culture towards an investigation of middle-aged black men, which until now has escaped academic scrutiny. The narratives contained in this text are foregrounded in the years respondents spent in Newham in East London, during a time when the area was ranked bottom of the available statistical indices for socioeconomics, health and education in Britain.

History is the key to understanding, and is best qualified to reward all research; therefore, Chapter 2 is concerned with constructing a historical framework by which the focal issues of this monograph can be positioned. This chapter also draws attention to the often-overlooked legacy of black presence in Britain, and highlights the pursuit of social justice that acted as a crucible for race relations during the Thatcher years. Chapter 3 introduces the focal characters within this text, and then focuses on the methodological processes undertaken to create it. Additionally it introduces the importance of issues such as black by black research and challenges assumptions such as 'It has all been done already; we know everything there is to know about the black minority in this country' (Phillips & Pugh, 2002:9). Chapters 4 and 5 discuss the topics of identity and masculinity respectively. They provide a conceptual insight into the lives of post-*Windrush*-generation men, and act as a prism through which additional factors can be examined. The attention-grabbing premise of the sexualisation of the black male is presented here, as well as a brief content analysis of film and music, and a discourse on media representations of black men.

The chapters that follow investigate experiences of black men in relation to societal institutions such as education, family configuration, criminal justice and religion. Chapter 6 explores the nature of the black family unit in modern Britain, highlighting the emergent themes gleaned from my investigation, such as domestic discipline and intergenerational conflict. Chapter 7 is concerned with education, beginning with a comparative account of education in the Caribbean and education in Britain. This chapter is predominantly sited in the 1970s and 1980s, as this was the period of compulsory education for those interviewed. Sport in school is touched upon, and the chapter concludes with the barbed issue of racism within education. Chapter 8 concentrates upon religion, opening with a condensed account of the sociology of religion and concluding by observing the manner in which postmodern religious beliefs such as Rastafari have had an impact on the collective identity of blacks in Britain. The focal point of Chapter 9 is crime. This chapter analyses issues such as criminal drift, regenerative shaming and desistance, as well as drug and alcohol use. The Conclusion (Chapter 10) sums up my key findings, significant emergent themes and recommendations for future research.

Notes

1 Training to become a London taxi driver. This lasts three to five years.
2 An annual austere work period, typically January to March, when cabbies are said to adopt frugal means of survival, such as a diet of kippers.
3 An apprenticed cabbie.
4 4 May 1979–28 November 1990.

5 Ex-Second World War troopships, which brought predominately Caribbean men, and a small number of Polish women, to Britain.
6 Five pence. Two 'bob' equals ten pence.

References

Banton, M. (1967) *Race Relations*, London: Tavistock.
Hall, S. (1973) *Encoding and Decoding in the Television Discourse*, Birmingham: Centre for Contemporary Cultural Studies.
Lamming, G. (1993) *In the Castle of My Skin*, Harlow: Longman.
Lamming, G. (1994) *The Emigrants*, Ann Arbor: University of Michigan Press.
Phillips, E. & Pugh, D. S. (2002) *How to Get a PhD*, Buckingham: Open University Press.
Pryce, K. (1979) *Endless Pressure*, Bristol: Bristol Classical Press.
Selvon, S. (1967) *Lonely Londoners*, London: Penguin.
Selvon, S. (1975) *Moses Ascending*, London: Penguin.
Sutcliffe, A. & Smith, R. (1974) *Birmingham 1939–1970*, Oxford: Oxford University Press.

Chapter 2

Historical context

History is key to understanding and context is king. This chapter therefore provides a usable historical framework within which much of the data gleaned from the field is presented. Moreover, in order to remain scrupulous and thorough, it is imperative that a robust and indomitable backcloth is established. Consequently, this chapter has several aims. The main objective is to provide a historical timeline for the portrayal and representation of blackness, particularly via the celebrated intellectualism of the Enlightenment period.[1] I will then chronicle black presence in Britain, and outline relevant historical events related to this, particularly in reference to episodes of social justice. I will conclude by examining the outcomes of these episodes on the lives of the post-*Windrush* generation, who are the primary concern of this text.

Unquestionably, there exists a small canon of sociological literature that speaks of black men in Britain. Equally unquestioned is that much of this work is presented through the eyes of those who are outside the population they observe: namely, white, middle-aged and often middle-class men, such as Cashmore (1984) for example. This can raise questions of positionality concerning those Du Bois (1978) refers to as 'car wash sociologists'. Glynn (2014) develops this by suggesting that research focused on black communities is often conducted by those who like to 'talk cricket from the boundary, but seldom face a fast bowler from the crease':

> I inhabit the world from which my constituents come. I am not talking about holding focus groups in comfy constructed spaces, or handing out questionnaires in the safety of the classroom, or sitting in the comfort of an office, tape recording someone who has signed up to your research. I'm talking about research that takes place in shopping centres, barber shops, bookies, car parks, street corners, and other locations within the confines of the inner cities.
>
> (Glynn, 2014:53)

It is important to highlight the parallels between debates surrounding the idea of race and the notable developments of feminist perspectives within the social sciences. For example, early feminists defined the social sciences as a discipline about men, for men, by men, which denied women the opportunity to tackle issues relevant and appropriate to their position in society (Smart, 1995). Similarly, we see studies of such topics as race and ethnicity often issuing from an exclusive and privileged few. Staples (1976) speaks here of race, but this of course can equally be ascribed to class, sexuality or gender:

> The problem of whites studying blacks is not unique to sociology or to the question of race. Intellectual elites have traditionally come from the group in control, and have tended to dominate the interpretation of the minority groups' behaviour. Thus, we find most studies of women have been by men, the middle class interpret lower-class behaviour, and Europeans develop the body of knowledge about Africans and Asians.
>
> (Staples, 1976:4)

Early sociologists, for the most part, placed what they called 'people of colour' outside their theoretical frameworks. The noted founding fathers of sociology, Comte and Spencer, made no obvious mention of blacks within their work. Moreover, no comprehensive analyses of blacks can be found within the core texts of celebrated commentators such as Marx, Weber and Durkheim. This scholarly omission allowed the eighteenth-century school of biological determinism to flourish within academic circles. Lombroso's insistence that dark skin is an indication of a chromosome imbalance, and a key indicator of criminal commission, for example, thrived unchallenged for many years.[2] Eze (1997) suggests that genetic deterministic theories such as those offered by Lombroso were in fact birthed from Enlightenment philosophers such as Hippocrates, Kant and Montesquieu:

> The Enlightenment's declaration of itself as 'The age of Reason' was predicated upon precisely the assumption that reason could historically only come to maturity in modern Europe, while the inhabitants of areas outside Europe, who were considered to be of non-European racial and cultural origins, were consistently described and theorised as rationally inferior and savage.
>
> (Eze, 1997:4)

Thinkers of this period habitually depicted blacks as highly sexualised and deviant brutes, who were devoid of reasoning or cerebral capacity (Fredrickson, 1971). This view, particularly of the black male, has prevailed for many years:

> When a knock is heard at the door a white woman shudders with nameless horror. The black brute is lurking in the dark. A monstrous beast crazed

with lust, his ferocity is almost demoniacal. A mad bull or tiger could scarcely be more brutal. A whole community frenzied with horror.

(Winston, 1901:108)

Prominent European and North American scholars, whose theories and philosophies lie at the heart of sociological thought, are the very same individuals who were responsible for disparaging assumptions regarding racial classifications. Immanuel Kant, for example, produced a number of works that made clear his opinion of Negroes:

In the hot countries the human being matures in all aspects earlier, but does not, however, reach the perfection of those in the temperate zones. Humanity is at its greatest perfection in the race of the whites. The yellow Indians do have a meagre talent. The Negroes are far below them and at the lowest point are a part of the American peoples.

(Kant, 1775, cited in Eze, 1997:66)

Similarly, the British philosopher David Hume states:

I am apt to suspect the Negroes and in general all the other species of men (for there are four or five different kinds), to be naturally inferior to the whites. There never was a civilised nation of any other complexion than white, nor even any individual eminent either in action or speculation. No ingenious manufactures amongst them, no arts, no sciences.

(Hume, cited in Greig, 1932:128)

Thinkers of the age stressed that 'the black' was devoid of rationality, and incapable of reason, rendering him absent in the hierarchical structure of humanity, and to be considered no more than a beast (Isaac, 2001). These eminent philosophers, despite openly commending the virtues of free thinking, and stressing the importance of liberty and empowerment of the individual, not only spoke but acted in direct contradiction to their own philosophies. For example, John Locke, the father of liberalism, invested heavily in human chattel through the Royal African Society (Morton, 2000). Moreover, the documented worldview of such scholars suggested that the moral code of the European is able to transform one from barbarity to civility. However, nature does not allow a corresponding transformation to occur among non-Europeans. Therefore 'the black' is perpetually depicted as beastlike, and assigned animalistic tendencies that are considered innate. This, Fanon suggests,

[h]as created a massive psycho-existential complex squarely located in the history of slavery and western colonialism. This political economic experience has impacted not only on the material social and economic lives of colonised people, but also on the language, culture and ultimately the

psyche. The historical experience of colonisation and subjugation and the contemporary experience of social, economic political marginalisation, led to a feeling of insignificance and to an insularity that becomes unbearable because the goals and standards of success in the white world are defined in ways which makes them impossible to achieve.

(Fanon, 1967, cited in Bowling & Phillips, 2002:72)

Such ideas have seeped into relatively recent sociological debate. See, for example, Herrnstein and Murray (1994), who suggest that blacks are innately less intelligent than other racial classifications, and as a result are predisposed to deviancy and ultimately criminality. All too frequently, an analysis of crime within sociological literature manifests a subtext that speaks of blacks as offenders, purely in relation to their engagement with enforcement agencies. This is an area of some concern for me as a lecturer in criminology and criminal justice, where I notice a number of modules with a specific focus on 'black criminality' built into curriculum designs, a focus that has a negative impact on black students, particularly males.

A forgotten history of black presence in Britain

The starting point of black presence in Britain is often situated around the epoch of the transatlantic trade in human chattel, commonly referred to as the African slave trade. However, as evidenced by historian Peter Fryer, 'There were Africans [blacks] in Britain before the English came here' (Fryer, 2010:132). A less-than exhaustive investigation reveals that a significant number of blacks were part of the Roman army that founded Londinium (London) in 43–50 CE, and outlines the sovereignty of the Roman emperor Septimius Severus, an African, who governed Britain between 193 and 211 (Birley, 1999; Jagessar, 2007). Moreover, artefacts that validate black presence have been found liberally scattered throughout Britain. One such location is the area surrounding Hadrian's Wall in Cumbria. Carvings known as 'Negro Heads' can be seen in the great hall in the London residence of the Archbishop of Canterbury at Lambeth Palace. Black residence in Britain between the First and Second World Wars is evidenced by a number of texts that explore the contribution of black people to the war effort and to the home front (Scobie, 1972; Noble, 1984; Sherwood, 1985; Bourne, 2010):

It has been estimated that there were at least 15,000 black and mixed race citizens of African, Caribbean, American and British backgrounds in England, Wales and Scotland when war was declared on 3 September 1939, but the figure could have been as high as 40,000. At the outbreak of war, the largest black communities were to be found in the Bute town (Tiger Bay) area of Cardiff in south Wales, Liverpool and the Canning Town and Custom House area of East London's dockland. In 1935 Nance Hare's survey of London's black population recorded the presence of 1500 black seamen and 250–300 working-class families with West Indian or African heads of households.

(Bourne, 2010:11)

It is undeniable that the infrastructure of modern European and North American societies was financed by the institution of chattel slavery that occurred around the Atlantic basin as early as 1440 (Williams, 1944; Rodney, 1973). This is a point which, owing to the logistical limits of space, will not be covered in depth within this chapter. However, in the interest of context it is necessary that the legacy of Britain's role in the institution of chattel slavery should be briefly outlined.

The economy of Britain continued to flourish beyond Wilberforce's petition for a ban on slave trading (the Slavery Trade Act, 1807), and the ensuing emancipation declaration (the Slave Abolition Act of 1833), which unfettered bondsmen throughout what was then known as the British West Indies. However, despite the lionisation of Wilberforce, Clarkson and the Clapham sect's parliamentarian lobbying for slavery reform, Britain was far from being the first European nation to abolish the chattel slave trade. The Danes, for example, decreed the abolition of the slave trade in 1792, over forty years before the British declaration of emancipation. Furthermore, historical documentation provides evidence suggesting that the enslavement of blacks continued in Britain long after the 1833 Act was passed. Records compiled by the African Society of London state that approximately 60,000 slaves were still being shipped across the Atlantic annually by Britain for significant periods (File & Power, 1981). Williams (1944) suggests that the profits from the transatlantic trade in slaves provided the manpower necessary to finance the Industrial Revolution. In order for industry to thrive, slave labour abroad and servitude at home were imperative, and although the majority of British-owned slaves were stationed in the West Indies, a small but visible number of black slaves were resident in Britain. However, as with the *Windrush* arrival centuries later, black people in Britain were neither acknowledged nor welcomed beyond the needs of servitude.

Enoch Powell[3] was not the first individual of prominence to call for the departure of blacks from Britain. Centuries before Powell's appointment to the position of Secretary of State, Casper Van Senden, an influential merchant, in 1596, under the reign of Elizabeth I, called for repatriation of African people from British soil, despite being aware that the monarch employed a number of black courtiers and maidservants on her staff. Although Queen Elizabeth dismissed Van Senden's call, she is quoted as stating:

Her Majestie, understanding that there are divers black moors brought into this realm, of which kinde of people there are already too manie, considering hows God has blessed this land with great increase of people of our own nation . . . whereas manie for wante of service and means to set them

on work fall on idleness and to great extremity. Her majestys pleasure is
that those kinde of people should be sent forth of the land.

(Dabydeen et al., 2010:146)

The monarch remained a strong advocate of the slave trade, demonstrated by her
mandate for a number of slave expeditions led by familiar figures such as Sir
Francis Drake and his cousin, the notorious brigand and buccaneer John Haw-
kins (File & Power, 1981). Her financial backing of such ventures legitimised
the British role in the trade of human chattel. Dabydeen et al. (2010) suggest
that between 1563 and 1569, she commissioned five slave-trading trips to West
Africa, which resulted in the capture of 3,000 human beings destined to become
units of labour to further the expansion of the British Empire. Centuries later, by
various deviations and detours, descendants of those captured, in a cruel twist of
irony, would be invited back to the shores of Britain, again to be units of labour.
However, on this occasion their task was to assist in re-establishing Britain's
role to, according to the lyricist James Thomson, 'rule the waves'.

The only way is Essex: the arrival of the *Empire Windrush*

> The *Windrush* sailed through a gateway of history, on the other side of which
> was the end of Empire and a wholesale reassessment of what it meant to be
> British.
>
> (Phillips & Phillips, 1998:6)

The most visible and arguably most significant Commonwealth migration to
Britain occurred late in the evening of 21 June 1948 at Tilbury dock in Essex,
with the arrival of an ex-German troopship, *The Monte Rosa*, more commonly
known as the *Empire Windrush*.

The cessation of the Second World War saw the British government attempt
to rebuild the superstructure of the nation, which had been ravaged by German
bombs. Due to shortage of labour in the public services sector, this was a huge
task, particularly with the imminent introduction of the National Health Service, which was to be instituted in July 1948. Politicians therefore turned to
the peoples of the Commonwealth for support. Recruitment campaigns offered
members of British colonies an opportunity to 'improve their lot', while simultaneously performing the noble task of rebuilding the 'Mother Country' to her
former glory and esteemed position. Envoys from the British government
embarked on widespread voluntary enlistment drives which inveigled many
ambitious but poor agricultural workers from the West Indies to Britain.

The experiences of these men and women who made this 5,000-mile journey
are beautifully told by novelists such as Dennis and Khan (2000) and Selvon
(1967, 1975). So noteworthy was the migration of West Indian peoples to Britain that it is documented not only in prose but also through poetry and song.

The material of the renowned Calypsonian Aldwyn 'Lord Kitchener' Roberts, for example, who arrived on *Empire Windrush*, provided a score for those who are said to have paid £28 for their passage and came to London in odd clothes and dazzling ties, clutching their cardboard grips. Those who walked the gang-plank at Tilbury laid the foundation for the following generations of blacks to arrive, but most importantly transformed British thinking about ideas of empire, race and citizenship. While the overwhelming number of those who disembarked from the *Empire Windrush* had been service personnel during the war, a sizable number was made up of those who had never journeyed from their place of birth, or even so much as met another West Indian beyond their own island.

The incomers had been socialised in the Caribbean through colonial schooling, which was firmly grounded in notions of empire. Therefore, any extended invitation from the Colonial Office was considered an honour, and an opportunity to exercise their instituted right to British citizenship.[4] Pryce (1979) mentions that the newly arrived held high Edwardian and Victorian values, and were proud to leave behind the 'backwardness' of the islands for a more advanced and sophisticated way of doing things. An example of this was the manner in which traditional linguistic codes of West Indian migrants such as Antillean Creole or Patois[5] were discouraged. Creole, in the Eastern Caribbean for example, was a byword for peasantry, and was considered by some to be ill mannered and a signature of ignorance. It was also regarded as unfit for purpose in the mother country; adoption of the Queen's (or King's) English was a much more desirable practice (Bennett-Coverley, 1966). Hubert, a pensioner from Trinidad, states:

> The flag was my flag, the king was my king and the language was my language. I didn't come to London to speak no Patwa. I didn't want to be like those old Coolies[6] who go around speaking in a way that nobody can understand, and make myself look stupid. I was an Englishman now, and had was [sic] to speak like an Englishman.
>
> (Hubert)

However, not all adopted this stance. Some looked upon the likes of Hubert with scorn, and thought it inappropriate for a West Indian to speak with a spurious English accent. For them this equated to a loss of their blackness. Cletus, also a pensioner, testifies that his estranged brother fell into this category:

> I have a brother who like to tell you how West Indian he is, and how much of a Caribbean man he is, but all the time we all just laughing at him because he forget all about back home and even how to speak patwa. He think he was a white man now he come to in England. There did have many here just like him, who think the white way is the right way – you know – the ice of the white man is colder.
>
> (Cletus)

For the peasant class West Indian, Britain was an example of James Hilton's imagined utopia of Shangri-la and an avenue to escape the Caribbean's griping urban and rural poverty. Arduous physical work was not strange to these men and women, who were often agricultural workers, and used to hewing sugar cane, and toiling banana work, in the depressed agricultural environment of the post-colonial West Indies. These West Indian migrants, like the Irish before them, performed the occupations for which the English were not suited either physically or temperamentally.

Poor living and working conditions, and poor pay, became a reality of British life for *Windrush* arrivals. Humbly, they adjusted themselves to their situation and cast their pride aside in an attempt to provide materially for their families. Despite poor pay and low status, the result was an honest wage, which was considered a mark of respectability, and being seen as respectable above all else was a crucial feature of West Indian cultural modality (Pryce, 1979; Monrose, 2017).

Acquiring and securing safe employment and an ordered income were challenging enough, but the most turbulent challenge facing the newly arrived immigrants was finding accommodation. Although some employment was made available by the British government, no arrangements were made for stable accommodation. This prompted the highly coloured, and in my opinion mythical, adage 'No Blacks, No dogs, No Irish' on signs affixed to windows adjacent to 'room to let' posters. Consequently, the newly arrived were forced to live in residences that in many cases were clearly unfit for habitation. Many commented that they were shocked at the poor standards of living that they experienced upon arrival. Cletus reflects upon his entrance to England:

> When I first get off the boat I was thinking that my brother would be there waiting for me dress up in top hat and thing, with a carriage, that will carry me to a big house with shag carpet and expensive ornaments. Nothing like that happen boy. London was colder than I ever dream a place could be. When I speak I see smoke – cold it was cold like that! A fella come meet us in an old truck, and take us to our new home. That night is in the bathroom I sleep – in a rusty bath pan amongst three other fellas. All the other places them in the house occupy. Boy I was shame. I get mammagise [fooled] into coming here and living like that, but what to do?
>
> (Cletus)

Failure to secure accommodation meant that the newcomers were open to the manipulative and exploitative schemes of unscrupulous landlords such as Peter Rachman.[7] Rachman was one of the few property developers who provided multi-occupancy accommodation for the newly arrived blacks (Davis, 2001). Many of his properties were of poor standard, and overpriced, but those without an abode had few other options. The problematic legacy of housing black people was not limited to West London (Ladbroke Grove), where Rachman's empire was centred. In East London, years after the demise of Rachmanism, we see similar concerns. For instance, in Newham, the housing stock was depleted by 60 per cent, due to the Blitz. This, coupled with an influx of migration to the area, meant that cramped living conditions were common:

> These properties are in an advanced state of dilapidation and decay. Hastily constructed for easy profit during the building boom of the Victorian and Edwardian era, housing here suffers from all sorts of defects. Normal Victorian houses were built with at least a slight damp proof to protect them, but many of the homes in Newham don't even have that: the top structures have gone, timbers were undersized and back additions were built with half brick, and not whole bricks. This is an east end phenomenon; you will never see it anywhere else in London.
>
> (Newham Monitoring Project, 1991:7)

In addition, the local housing sector was often reluctant to accommodate West Indians, for it caused resentment amongst the established white tenants, some of whom even refused to pay their rent if a black lessee became an occupant. This forced blacks into the private housing sector, which in a very short time increased multi-occupancy in already overcrowded properties with unkempt structures, which in some cases were clearly dangerous. A solution to this was for them to pool their finances in order to afford to purchase their own property (similar to the 'partner draw',[8] which still exists within some black communities today). However, this too was fraught with difficulties, as realtors refused to sell homes to blacks: We have instructions from white owners that property must not on any account be sold to coloureds of any kind (Pryce, 1979:180).

To navigate this, some accepted assistance from supportive non-West Indian friends who took on the responsibility of securing a mortgage in their name, so a property could be purchased:

> It was an Irish friend of mine called Brendan who took out a mortgage for me to buy my first house for me in 1960. He himself knew the things that we had to go through and stood for us. Not all white people gave black people a hard time you know. There were some that treated us good and lived with us well, especially the Irish.
>
> (Donald)

Commonwealth migration from the West Indies continued at a steady pace until the late 1950s, when over 20,000 West Indian migrants were arriving in Britain every year. However this induced a new era of political intolerance and public indifference to black people, thanks to the introduction of the 1962

Commonwealth Immigration Act, which was designed to restrict Common-wealth migration to Britain:

> [A]nd this sort of thing was happening at a time when the English people starting to make rab about how too much West Indians coming to the country: this was a time when any corner you turn, is ten to one you bound to bounce up a spade. In fact the boys all over London, it ain't have a place that you wouldn't find them, and big discussion going on in parliament about the situation.
>
> (Selvon, 1967:24)

The socio-economic history of East London

The place that would become London, the centre of world trade and the pinnacle of the greatest empire ever seen, has been populated since the Ice Age, when people scavenged a living in the Thames Valley. The river was far broader and shallower then than it is today, and, without its artificial banks and walls, was more like a lake dotted with small islands (O'Neil, 2000:3).

London's East End historically consists of areas of settlement surrounding the walls of the river Lea – typically what we now know as Tower Hamlets. East London is a byword for cheap housing, poor health, exotic immigrants, stench, cheap labour and of course, crime. Prior to industrialisation, the area today known as Newham comprised a small cluster of villages and hamlets scattered around the rivers Lea, Roding and Thames, with the southernmost part of Epping Forest providing the fourth border of this quadrangular enclosure.

According to Anglo-Saxon Charter 958, the area was referred to as Hamme, which, in Anglo-Saxon Germanic inflected language or Old English, is defined as a portion of dry land positioned between rivers or marshland. In the twelfth century, Hamme was divided into two sections, West Hamme and East Hamme (West Ham and East Ham). It was part of Essex until 1965, when, along with North Woolwich, it became part of the administrative boundary of the newly formed county of Greater London. Historically Newham's role shortly after the Industrial Revolution was to provide municipal manpower to serve the needs of the administrative hub of the British Empire, the City of London. A large number of Irish, who formed part of the British military after the Battle of Waterloo, settled in England and acted as the manpower of a newly industrial-ised Britain, particularly in the construction of canals, railways and docks[9] (Gaskell, 1833; Winder, 2013).

Toxic times

In the 1970s and 1980s, Newham was a dark and dismal place. A number of the once grand residential buildings in the north of the borough in Forest Gate, where I grew up, stood dilapidated and derelict many years after the Blitz. The south of the borough was worse. Due to the closure of the docks and factories, vast parts of the area became barren wastelands. In Beckton, for example, the largest gas works in Europe closed in 1969, leaving nearly 600 acres of land unoccupied. Ragged children and dogs were left to play amongst the rubble and decay that became a lasting feature of areas such as Canning Town, Custom House and Silvertown:

> I grew up in West Silvertown and that was considered posh. We used to build camps and all sorts of things on the bombsites. We'd find some really gruesome things when we played down by the river near the docks. It was exciting but very scary at the same time.
>
> (Terry)

Arguably, Newham at this time was not dissimilar to Mayhew's depictions of Victorian London, which identify a number of verifiable indicators of social deprivation (Mayhew, 1962). Charles Booth's socio-economic maps of the 1880s, in which the borough was regarded as the most deprived part of London, seemed relevant a century later (Booth, 1889). Linked to this deprivation was the promiscuous criminality that was an established feature of the area's informal (and sometimes formal) economy. Some clergymen regarded it as '[t]he worst parish in the diocese, inhabited mainly by a criminal population' (O'Neil, 2000:67). Locals strove by working to earn a living, but many had given up trying to find work and resorted to theft. Of Newham the social exclusion unit stated: 'people or areas [of Newham] suffer from a combination of linked problems such as unemployment, poor skills, low incomes, poor housing, high crime environments, bad health, poverty and family breakdown' (Social exclusion unit, 1998; 69 in Gunter, 2010:26).

Endurance in Newham involved navigating a hard way of life, which often meant living by one's wits and adopting innovative techniques for providing sustenance and shelter (Hobbs, 1988, 2013; Monrose, 2016). In fact Newham attracted the attention of a number of prominent historians, novelists and social reformers such as Walter Besant, Keir Hardie and Charles Dickens, who described West Ham in the following terms:

> A place of refuge for offensive trades . . . Canning Town is the child of the Victoria docks. The condition of this place and its neighbour prevents the steadier class of mechanics from residing in it. They go from their work to Stratford or to Plaistow. Many select such a dwelling place because they are already debased below the point of enmity to filth; poor labourers live there, because they cannot afford to go farther, and there become debased.
>
> (Dickens, 1857, in Armstrong et al., 2014:23)

This said, the strong, cohesive sense of community that existed within the area remains one of the more celebrated and enduring aspects of East End culture:

> If I can explain it like this: in them times, the community policed itself. They looked out for one another, so in your own little community, you made sure that nothing too bad happened.
>
> (O'Neil, 2000:87)

> One time, Mum lent the family over the road a pair of Dad's shoes. There was a wonderful feeling of belonging in that street. People would never close their doors on you.
>
> (O'Neil, 2000:86)

The legacy of newly built council properties that were hastily erected to replace the old and dilapidated housing stock in order to accommodate the expanding population is well known. Ronan Point, like the more recent disaster of Grenfell Tower in Ladbroke Grove, remains an example of the undependable administration of municipal high-density housing within environs increasingly being inhabited by the poor and newly arrived.[10]

A widespread lack of public consultation on a number of significant housing issues was left unchallenged in Newham during the 1970s. I witnessed this first hand, having grown up in badly designed accommodation, with inadequate safety provisions (a kitchen built next to the main entrance of the home, for example). My family moved from the south of Newham to a relatively newly constructed council estate in the north of the borough in 1974. Our block was adjacent to the Barking–Gospel Oak railway line in Forest Gate (commissioned by Sir Courtenay Warner as the Tottenham–Forest Gate railway in 1894). Freight trains thundered past so often that we'd fail to notice them. Our home shook incredibly when this happened, so that our conversations would be disturbed. Along with the noise and sooty emissions of the diesel engines, trains were said to be transporting nuclear waste throughout the night. An elderly resident who lived in the flat below ours often complained ardently about the threat of radioactive poisoning, but her protests didn't resonate with other residents. I suspect some were simply happy to have a seemingly safe place to live, which was some distance away from the ever-present violent racism in the south of the borough that we had escaped from – though in retrospect, it is uncomfortable knowing one was exposed every day to the dangers of nuclear waste.

However, concerns such as these are part of the legacy of environmental abuses that have taken place in East London since industrialisation. For example, the 1844 Metropolitan Building Act restricted noxious industrial waste from being used within London boundaries, but did not include Newham (then West Ham) as it stood outside the legislated perimeter and was considered a 'depository of nuisances' (Bermant, 1975:42).

White flight

By the mid-1970s, life in Britain had become increasingly politically charged, particularly with respect to race and immigration. Resentment of black presence grew to unprecedented heights, and we witnessed the re-emergence of extreme right-wing political groups such as the National Front, the Young National Front and the British Movement. The perceived threat of 'coloureds taking over' inflamed British sensibilities on migration, often grabbed headlines and elicited comments from members of the British public:

> While I have no dislike of the West Indian, I think it is time that they went back to their own country. After all they demanded independence. Let them now go back and enjoy it. What about our own countrymen who are in dire need through unemployment? The West Indian has their own country which should look after its own. Let councillors do the same here. First see that our own people are fed and housed. They cannot run off to Jamaica and get a job.
>
> (*Bristol Echo*, cited in Pryce, 1979:180)

The 1980s became a decade of huge social displacement in Newham, because of the privatisation of utility providers and the decline of manufacturing: 'The long-established social order of neighbourhoods fractured as dock workers and their families took their severance pay and moved out of London, taking with them a fierce local patriotism based upon the everyday realities of class antagonism' (Hobbs, 2013:93).

Deindustrialisation, as well as the newly implemented policies such as 'Right to Buy', resulted in the established, once white population of the East End slowly departing from the area in order to seek employment and set up homes elsewhere:[11]

> This sale of public housing overheated the housing market, and resulted in working-class council tenants buying their homes at a massive discount before selling at a profit and heading for London's periphery, which, combined with deindustrialisation, effectively drained working-class London of much of its human capital, as well as its cumulative memory.
>
> (Hobbs, 2013:93)

This was the official line offered for the geographical demographical shift, but the unofficial line of 'white flight', as we will see, held an alternative subtext. As well as depressed local employment opportunities, the increase in visible immigrant settlement fuelled a heightened level of political disenchantment amongst many whites, prompting their exodus from areas with supposedly high immigrant residence. White families who could afford to resettled in outlying areas. Others, less well off, moved to cheaper, newly built communities in areas of South Essex and North Kent where property was not only more affordable but, more importantly, free from 'foreigners':

Nobody wanted to live next door to blacks, Kenny, that was the worst thing that could happen to you and your family. You know what they say, you shouldn't mix your whites with your coloureds.

(Terry)

I love it here, Ken. There's none out here. This is proper England, only people like us! Well, you know what I mean, no offence or nothing.

(Phil)

I loved our old house in East Ham, it was lovely. You had West Ham [football club] around the corner, good pubs, and everyone knew each other until the coloureds moved in. Don't get me wrong, your normal coloureds was OK, they were nice people, it was just the smell. The smell would seep through the walls, and there were so many of them in one house we just had to move.

(Peter the Bookie)

There are too many stinks of foreign cooking. You can say I'm racist if you like. The lifts are filthy because of their spitting and urine, and they leave rubbish everywhere.

(Dench et al., 2006:173)

Deep-seated sentiments such as these, as we will see in the following section, led to episodes of social resistance and uprising that essentially shaped the manner in which a portrait of the post-*Windrush* generation can be constructed, and the manner in which black British identity has been developed.

'A bloody good hiding': resistance and riot

Race riots in North America raise an anxious question from some people living in Britain's immigrant areas. Could it possibly happen here? Some people who know race relations think the answer is yes.

(*The Sunday Times*, 30 July 1967)

Race has often been an understated issue in Britain, and something the British 'don't like talking about'. In this section, however, I will point out that race *is* something that we in Britain need to talk about, particularly in assessing episodes of social resistance within our borders.

The enormous influence of racism and racialisation in shaping the cultural and political identity of black people in Britain cannot be underestimated.

Racially motivated attacks upon both the black mind and body have been perpetuated for as long as black people have been present in Britain. The racist
killing of Kelso Cochrane in 1959 occurred decades before the death of Stephen Lawrence in 1993. The criminal investigations into both these incidents,
and numberless others before, after and in between, have yielded the same
conclusion – the failure of the criminal justice system to secure a timely conviction. Although the enquiry into the murder of Stephen Lawrence led to an
acknowledgement that racism exists at alarmingly high levels in British institutions, did we really need to wait until 1999 for Lord Macpherson to validate
this, when Lord Scarman (1981, 1986) had made it explicit many years previously that there was a dire need to reform and overhaul the manner in which
the police and other institutions engage with black communities?

Civil unrest in Britain is not something new: it is well documented and has
been discussed at length by a number of social historians such as Clive Elmsley
and Henry Mayhew. Unlike incidents involving race, however, such incidents
are habitually framed within the public imagination as disputes, demonstrations
or at their very worst skirmishes. An example is the representation of the carnage that blighted towns such as Carlisle, Stockton, Wellington, Telford, North
Shields, Newcastle and Sunderland in the 1990s: the events were not classified
as riots but merely as heavy incidents of antisocial behaviour. In contrast, similar incidents of social unrest that occur in heavily populated minority ethnic
areas transcend from 'disturbances' to being labelled full-scale race riots.[12]
Observe the manner in which the riots in Toxteth in Liverpool, and years later
in Burnley in Lancashire, were presented (Lea, 2002). The thinly veiled subtext
that typically lies beneath the definition of such events becomes transparent to
those who can decipher the cryptic inscriptions of the media's propaganda
machine, which make these events seem as if they were only about poor
policing, when in truth they were equally about racial discrimination. Suffice to
say that, in the imagination of the British news media, the majority group do
not riot – minority ethnic groups do.

The earliest documented violent conflict of note involving black people in
Britain occurred in Cardiff in 1919. The 'Cardiff Negroland Conflicts' were
the first mass black declaration of resistance to the violent racism they were
subject to. After the First World War, Britain experienced heightened levels of
unemployment and homelessness, compounded by poor living conditions. As
is common at such times, those of visible difference were held to account and
blamed for the economic demise of the nation (Dabydeen et al., 2010; Fryer,
2010). As a result of this indictment, racially motivated attacks took place in
a number of British port towns such as Liverpool and Exeter, but more
potently in Cardiff. Areas such as Butetown (Tiger Bay), where significant
numbers of blacks resided, experienced disturbances. Groups of whites, led,
ironically, by armed, 'non-visible' Australian immigrant soldiers, mobilised,
and carried out attacks on the lodgings and homes of what were mainly black
ex-servicemen.

In August 1958, a mere ten years after the arrival of the *Windrush*, we see the unfolding of a series of events that acted as a barometer for measuring attitudes to race in Britain. Disturbances in Notting Hill created a momentum that placed race at the centre of political debate for years to come: 'Almost from the moment of the first stages of arrival of black workers in the UK, they were perceived both within and outside government as a problem' (Solomos, 1988:30).

Blacks, Solomos (1988) argues, were constructed into bearers of ascribed unhelpful characteristics that would act as a threat to British society. Thus, the now infamous Powellite prophesy of an impending racial civil war created a lasting image of the black male as a new folk devil – a label that, as we will see, accompanied and firmly attached itself to the post-*Windrush* generation.

The next section will go on to explore the impact of Margaret Thatcher's government on cementing a political legacy soiled with civil unrest and racial tension throughout Britain.

'Thatcher, Thatcher, milk snatcher': the impact of Thatcherism on race relations and policing

Even before her appointment as Prime Minister in May 1979, Margaret Hilda Thatcher was courting controversy. As Secretary of State for Education in 1970–74, she revoked free milk allowances in schools, an act that justifiably singled her out for harsh criticism. However, this was a mere precursor of hard-line legislative measures she was to adopt within her eleven-year premiership. Her legacy as one of the longest-serving British Prime Ministers of the twentieth century will be remembered by many for the sheer number of violent civil disorders that the country witnessed under her watch. In addition, the new powers that Thatcher extended to the police transformed the face of British policing beyond all recognition.

With Thatcher at the helm, Britain witnessed a steady demise of what was deemed to be, and cherished as, the 'golden age' of British policing. Community policing and policing by consensus were curtailed, particularly in urban areas. With her implementation of target hardening, and her deployment of military trained personnel into key positions of police authority, the cohesive and co-operative relationship between communities and law enforcement was destined to break down (Newburn, 1990; Davies et al., 1998). The police, for some, were no longer considered a service to serve the public. Under Thatcher, they became a quasi-military organisation, in place to keep the masses subservient and ordered. An inevitable result of this militarisation of the police was the criminalisation of black and minority ethnic communities. For example, in 1987, Metropolitan Police Commissioner Kenneth Newman[13] outrageously insisted that areas inhabited by 'ethnics' should be policed as if policing terrorists:

There is one thing that policing terrorism has in common with policing ethnic ghettoes. Policing activities must be accomplished by social and

economic measures and the policies of the police and civil administration
must be co-ordinated with a coherent strategy.
(Metropolitan Police Commissioner Newman, 1987, cited in Rose, 1992:37)

Numerous social maladies fouled Thatcher's tenure, but the Brixton riots in
1981 had huge ramifications which changed the face of race relations in Britain for ever. 'Brixton '81' was sparked by the re-introduction of the antiquated
Vagrancy Act of 1824,[14] which deemed it illegal for 'a suspected person or
reputed thief to frequent or loiter in a public place, with the intent to commit
an arrestable offence' (HMSO 1824, C83, section 4). This allowed the police
to stop and search whoever they wished on the basis of suspicion, and became
known as the infamous 'sus law', which, due to its misuse, led to the events
of April 1981. In 1978, before the commencement of her premiership,
Thatcher had made a speech upon which the name of the police initiative in
Lambeth, SWAMP 81,[15] is said to have been based:

> People are really afraid that this country might be rather swamped by
> people from a different culture. The British character has done so much
> for democracy, our land has done so much throughout the world, that if
> there is any fear that it might be swamped, people are going to react and
> be rather hostile to those coming in.
>
> (Margaret Thatcher, *World in Action*, Granada TV, 1978)

SWAMP 81 led to almost 1,000 people being stopped and searched in six
days. Of this number, only 170 people were arrested and a small number
charged with an indictable offence. This led to the events of 10 April, which
still produce a lasting image within the psyche of the British public of racialised urban unrest. The 280 police who were injured, and the extensive carnage,
in a normally peaceful but horribly deprived part of London seemed to be the
price paid for ignoring the pleas from community spokespeople, elders and
youth workers, who in the aftermath quietly murmured to all who would
listen, 'We told you so', referring to the inevitable results of poor policing.

Attacks on police officers were carried out with an assortment of weapons, not just sticks, bottles and stones but home-made incendiary devices
such as Molotov cocktails. Rose (1992) suggests this was the first time
petrol bombs were used against the police in mainland Britain. Widespread
looting and arson ensued, leaving the area in meltdown, and the egos of
those responsible for policing deflated. The Brixton riots, like many of the
other disturbances, were shows of resistance by those who considered themselves to be victimised and pushed to the margins of British society. The
events reminded those within government that all was not well with either
race relations or policing. Attempts at racial integration had failed miserably,
and instead of black communities feeling more integrated into British life,

the opposite had occurred, leaving black youths of the post-*Windrush* generation more marginalised than ever:

> The traditions of anti-colonialism dormant in the first generation of immigrants are resuscitated in the youth of the second generation. Thus areas such as Railton Road in Brixton or St Pauls in Bristol represent the toehold of colonial people fighting back against imperialism. The frontline is a colony within the host country. The culture that has grown up there is the vanguard of Afro-Caribbean culture – it is a culture of survival which every now and then breaks out into open resistance.
>
> (Lea & Young, 1984:119)

Britain's economic depression at this time did little to help. Figures on the socio-economic position of black people in Britain made stark reading. Britain was already in economic decline by 1981, and, although the country was witnessing a falling population, there was evidence of both housing shortages and high unemployment. Black communities throughout Britain felt the brunt of this (Bowling & Phillips, 2002). Black youths then occupied the same labour market position as the *Windrush* arrivals, if they managed to secure employment at all, and were financially dependent on the state. Due to cuts in public spending, recreational facilities became increasingly sparse, which meant that the few public spaces where black youths felt safe to congregate became labelled 'frontlines' (Monrose, 2016).[16] These spaces were often characterised as symbolic locations where an illegal street economy of drug dealing, prostitution, drug usage, fencing and all manner of illicit activity took place:

> Locations where unemployed youths – often black youths – congregate; where the sale and purchase of drugs, the exchange of stolen property and illegal drinking and gaming is not unknown. The youths regard these symbolic locations as their territory. Police are viewed as intruders, the symbolic authority . . . they equate closely with the criminal rookeries of Dickensian London.
>
> (Rose, 1992:32)

Black eateries, community centres, parties and even places of worship were regularly raided by police on so called 'coon hunting' expeditions (Solomos, 1988). Blanket stop-and-search tactics adopted by the police against society's powerless, disenfranchised underclass further added to their sense of alienation. The subsequent enquiry by Lord Scarman into the disturbances in Brixton awakened the British public to the unprecedented depths to which relations between the police and black communities had plummeted, and made it clear that the events of 1981 did not occur by accident, but as a direct consequence of non-action by successive governments.

Lipsky and Olsen (1977) provide a model in which earlier 'race riots' in North America can be compared to the social unrest in the UK. They argue that the primary aim of political rule within the context of civil unrest is to make sure that law and order is re-established upon the streets. The second aim, they suggest, is to minimise the political impact of these violent clashes, and create an illusion that these uprisings were simply forms of random, wanton and meaningless violence. Finally, they propose that if injustice is established, then a guarantee of some form of remedial action should be presented. Scarman's 1981 report ticked all these boxes and, as expected, deftly deflected the primary blame of the conflict from all but those who were truly responsible – clearly, the police and legislators. Years later, however, Scarman himself claimed that the language used by the state in reference to the events of Brixton was considerably different from the language used by the rioters. This is significant as it leaves the final analysis of the events of Brixton open to inexact conclusions, particularly in the representations of policing black communities disseminated in the news media. The orientation of Scarman's report suggests that the relationship between the command of the state and the black communities had crystallised into a relationship between police and black youth.

Scarman concluded his report by recommending that a balance needed to be established by enforcement that lay somewhere between crime prevention and civil tranquillity. Crucially, he pointed out that identifiable factors in the policing of black communities would lead to a situation in which violent protest and confrontation were likely to occur. Even so, his report failed to explicitly identify why black people were so angry with the type of policing that they were subject to. Nevertheless, had the recommendations made in his first report been taken seriously and implemented, maybe further disorder such as the Tottenham riots in 1985 might not have occurred.

As with Brixton, the Broadwater Farm riots in Tottenham highlighted the problems between black people and the police. The disturbances surrounding events on the Broadwater Farm estate reignited the fuse of friction not just between the police and black communities, but also the news media. Gilroy (1987) suggests that the media relished portraying black youth as a high crime group, whose criminality was an expression of their distinctive culture. Bowling and Phillips (2002), like Gilroy, argue that the riots of 1985 re-established issues of race, crime and disorder in a more expansive manner within the media than the reporting of the unrest of 1981 ever did. Lord Gifford's inquiry (1986) into the disturbances in Tottenham reminded us that the relationship between the police and black communities had a volatile history, which neither side had made steps to improve. The report states:

> Witness after witness to our inquiry spoke of the indignities which they have suffered at the hands of police officers for no other reason than they were black.
>
> (Lord Gifford's report, cited in Rose, 1992:40)

There is neither time nor space to fully explore the tragic events that took place in Tottenham on the night of 6 October 1985. The conclusion of these events is well known. PC Keith Blakelock lost his life, apparently by being 'hacked to pieces', and vast numbers of police were injured and hospitalised. During the aftermath of the riots, the Labour MP Bernie Grant stated, 'They [the police] received a bloody good hiding' (Rose, 1992:78).

Enquiries after Brixton and Tottenham saw an almost apologetic attempt by institutional bodies to combat racial discrimination by encouraging greater black participation in public life. The high-spending policies of the Greater London Council (GLC), under the leadership of Ken Livingstone, allowed black artistic expression to thrive in London. Funds were made available for black-led community initiatives and new forms of racial awareness to emerge. There was also an overdue acknowledgement of the black British intellectual class such as 'The Birmingham School'.[17] Black personalities became fixtures within the media, and we saw blacks entering local politics and establishing black sections within the Labour Party for the first time: Russell Profitt, Paul Boateng, Diane Abbott, Bernie Grant.

Nonetheless, despite these assumed advances, the vast majority of blacks in Britain, who were not members of the new black petit bourgeoisie, remained firmly positioned as chronic members of Thatcher's underclass. This was typi-fied by the post-*Windrush* generation, who were born in Britain but held little stake in British society. Unlike their parents they were not simply passing through, they were here to stay, and as a consequence had no other choice than to attempt to engage with Britain's class/race structure.

The 1990s saw public funds being revoked nationally, and in London the demise of the GLC. This hit the black communities of London hard, as they had become reliant upon government funding to thrive. Moreover, Thatcherism had become synonymous with individualism, and with this came the end of the politicised solidarity that existed among minority ethnic groups who had joined forces to mobilise against injustice. Politically Asians were no longer considered black, and issues of ethnic difference and dichotomy begin to mani-fest themselves. We now noticed the emergence of a developed narrative of cultural identity amongst second-generation British-born blacks. Members of this group, who ardently considered themselves West Indian despite being born in Britain, began to slowly accept the realisation that Britishness was not quintessentially tied to whiteness. Being black could also mean that one could be British, without just relying on being a British representative in sport – although, as we shall see, these ideas are far more complex than might be supposed.

Conclusion

This chapter has established the historical context whereby the men who form part of this study can be properly understood. It is critical that a rigorous engagement with the past should be presented, as this offers an understanding of the legacy of discrimination and intolerance that black people in Britain have faced. The stance adopted by philosophers of the Enlightenment is of key importance, as it is from their reasoning that definitions and subsequent attitudes to race have developed. A presentation of black presence in Britain also unearths a forgotten history, and acts as a reminder that blacks have been a part of British society for centuries, and have often experienced challenges to their acceptance, in spite of directed legalisation.[18] These concerns came to a climax during the 1980s in a series of insurrections, in the aftermath of which matters of race and policing were debated with increased precision, and blacks in Britain began to question their cultural identity within the political arena. This arguably assisted in the formation and emergence of a black intellectual class, opening dialogues about cultural awareness and finally making race something that the British *had* to talk about. Moreover, from the ashes of the 1981 and 1985 insurrections arose what could be described as a black renaissance, wherein, against the grain and quite unexpectedly, the aesthetic of blackness became celebrated within British culture.

Acting as a necessary backdrop to the entire text, this chapter has shown just how complex the difficulties facing West Indians have been since the *Windrush* arrival some seventy years ago. Difficulties in employment and accommodation were the main challenges, but they were willing in part to accept them as they were only passing through. Rather, it is their offspring, those on whom this text focuses, who have faced lasting difficulties. Issues such as political marginalisation, violence, poverty, institutionalised racism and an absence from the British class structure formed the pillars of a society that the post-*Windrush* generation were forced to negotiate without escape. The stage is now set for the arrival of the black men upon whose lives this study is based.

Notes

1 The Age of Enlightenment, or the Enlightenment period, is a term used to describe a time in European philosophy and cultural life, centred in the eighteenth century, when reason was advocated as the primary source of and legitimacy for authority.

2 Scientists seek rational explanations of phenomena, because with understanding of the mechanics comes the ability to reform, revamp or reject. Being influenced by Darwinism, Lombroso looked to apply this belief system to crime. In order to determine what made men criminal, he hypothesised that criminality can be reflected in physical characteristics, including factors such as race.

3 John Enoch Powell was a Conservative MP between 1950 and 1974. He was best known for his 'Rivers of Blood' speech in 1968, which focused on immigration. But this was not the central theme of the speech, as is widely reported. Powell's thesis was a direct critique of the Labour government's introduction of the 1968 Race Relations Act, which deemed it illegal to refuse housing, employment and public service to individuals on the basis of colour, race or ethnicity. Whilst the Act was subsequently passed and Powell had his parliamentary position revoked, his eloquence afforded him widespread white working-class support, for example from

dockers and meat packers. However, in the eyes of many others, particularly those in minority communities, his lasting legacy is one of bigotry and a name synonymous with racism.

4 The post-1945 Labour government's programme of recruiting displaced persons to work in a number of industries and services deemed essential for economic recovery and suffering from labour shortages.

5 Creole or Patwa is a natural language developed from the mixing of parent languages.

6 A historical term for manual labourers or indentured slaves from Asia during the nineteenth and early twentieth centuries. It is also a racial slur or ethnic nickname for people of Asian descent.

7 Landlord/property developer. In order to maximise the rent from his properties, he is said to have driven out the mostly white sitting tenants in Notting Hill, who had statutory protection against high rent increases, and then to have packed the properties with recent immigrants. New tenants did not have the same protection under the law as the sitting tenants had possessed, and could be charged any amount Rachman proposed. Most of the new tenants were West Indian immigrants who had no choice but to accept the high rents, as it was difficult for them to obtain housing in London at the time. Indeed, Rachman's initial reputation, which he even promoted in the media, was as someone who could help provide accommodation for immigrants who would otherwise find it difficult.

8 Credit union system deemed illegal.

9 The docks acted as the gateway to the wealth of the nation, as it was here that commodities and raw materials arrived from the Commonwealth. The sheer expanse of the docks meant that a considerable workforce was necessary to keep it functioning effectively. To be a dock worker during the postwar years was considered a lucrative career move, which, once entered, would become employment for life. However, dock work was reserved for white English working men, whose heritage lay in the local community. Employment was often passed on from father to son, or to other extended family members and/or close associates, and it was unusual for those outside these degrees of separation to be granted this opportunity. Consequently the newly arrived blacks who resided in dock areas found it difficult to secure work there. Instead many were employed in the numerous factories and foundries situated around the docks, in companies such as Ford, Tate & Lyle and Fray Bentos (Benyon, 1974).

10 A 22-storey tower block in Canning Town in Newham, East London, which collapsed on 16 May 1968, two months after it had opened. A gas explosion blew out some load-bearing walls, causing the collapse of one entire corner of the building. The spectacular nature of the failure (caused by both poor design and poor construction) led to a loss of public confidence in high-rise residential buildings, and major changes in UK building regulations.

11 Right to Buy was part of the 1980 Housing Act, and was one of the first significant policy reforms introduced by the Thatcher government. Right to Buy forced local authorities to sell their properties on request to existing tenants at a discount, and despite controversy and opposition, 90,000 properties were sold in the year of its inception.

12 The term 'race riots' suggests that a battle takes place between those of one race and those of another, that is to say, black vs. white. But this is not always accurate. O'Neil (2000) stresses that as early as 1806 there was inter-group fighting amongst Lascars, Chinese and Irishmen in East London, which is widely regarded by scholars as the first time Britain witnessed race riots.

13 Metropolitan Police Commissioner Sir Kenneth Newman's occupational history lay in having spent several years as chief of operations in the Royal Ulster

Constabulary, through some of its more turbulent times. It therefore came as no surprise that some of the operational tactics he implemented whilst in command of the Met were based on his experiences in Northern Ireland. Newman was responsible for bringing plastic bullets to the streets of London, and also held office when CS gas was deployed for the first time outside Northern Ireland. He was clearly an advocate of militarised and heavy-handed policing.

14 The 1824 Vagrancy Act was introduced to deal with specific problems in England following the Napoleonic Wars.

15 SWAMP 81: Thatcher's new government encouraged the police to impose quasi-military tactics and a 'heavy heavy' approach to policing, under the guise of proactive policing. This began with the introduction of the notorious 'sus' law. Theoretically this was an attempt to curb crime, but in practical terms it was to prove highly contentious as well as hugely counterproductive. The aim of the law in simple terms was to apprehend a suspect on the suspicion of being either to, or from, or in the process of, committing an act of crime. This of course overwhelmingly targeted a large number of black males, who were regularly stopped and searched in the course of their daily movements. This should not be surprising as black men fall into the category often referred to as 'police property' – a term that includes many of society's marginalised groups such as the homeless, prostitutes, alcoholics and the working class.

16 Inner-city areas labelled by enforcement agents as rife with criminal activity.

17 The Centre for Contemporary Cultural Studies, founded by Professor Richard Hoggart at Birmingham University.

18 The Race Relations Act 1965 was the first legislation in the UK to address racial discrimination. The Act outlawed discrimination on the grounds of colour, race or ethnic or national origins in public places. The Race Relations Act 1968 was a British Act of Parliament making it illegal to refuse housing, employment or public services to a person on the grounds of colour, race or ethnic or national origins.

References

Armstrong, G., Giulianotti, R. & Hobbs, D. (2014) *Policing the 2012 London Olympics: Legacy and Social Exclusion*, London & New York: Routledge.

Bennett-Coverley, L. (1966) *Jamaican Song and Story*, New York: Dover Publications.

Benyon, H. (1974) *Working for Ford*, London: Allen Lane & Penguin.

Bermant, C. (1975) *London's East End: Point of Arrival*, London: Eyre Methuen.

Birley, A. (1999) *Septimius Severus: The African Emperor*, London: Routledge.

Booth, C. (1889) *Labour and Life of the People*, London: Williams & Norgate.

Bourne, S. (2010) *Mother Country: Britain's Black Community on the Home Front 1939–1945*, Stroud: The History Press.

Bowling, B. & Phillips, C. (2002) *Racism, Crime and Justice*, Harlow: Longman.

Cashmore, E. (1984) *The Rastafarians*, London: Minority Rights Group.

Dabydeen, D., Gilmore, M. & Jones, C. (2010) *Oxford Companion to Black British History*, Oxford: Oxford University Press.

Davies, M., Croall, H. & Tyrer, J. (1998) *An Introduction to the Criminal Justice System in England and Wales*, Harlow: Longman.

Davis, J. (2001) *Rents and Race in 1960s London: New Light on Rachmanism*, Oxford: Oxford University Press.

Dench, G., Gavron, K. & Young, M. (2006) *The New East End: Kinship, Race & Conflict*, London: Profile Books.

Dennis, F. & Khan, N. (2000) *Voices of the Crossing*, London: Serpent's Tail.

Du Bois, W. E. B. (1978) *On Sociology and the Black Community*, Chicago: The University of Chicago Press.

Eze, C. (1997) *Race and the Enlightenment: A Reader*, Oxford: Blackwell.

Fanon, F. (1967) *Black Skin, White Masks*, New York: Grove Press.

File, N. & Power, C. (1981) *Black Settlers in Britain 1555–1958*, London: Heinemann.

Fredrickson, M. (1971) *The Black Image in the White Mind*, New York: Harper & Row.

Fryer, P. (2010) *Staying Power: The History of Black People in Britain*, London: Pluto.

Gaskell, P. (1833) *The Manufacturing Population of England, Its Moral, Social and Physical Conditions, and the Changes Which Have Arisen from the Use of Steam Machinery: With an Examination of Child Labour*, London: Baldwin & Cradock.

Gifford, L. (1986) *The Broadwater Farm Inquiry*, London: Karia Press.

Gilroy, P. (1987) *There Ain't No Black in the Union Jack: The Cultural Politics of Race and Nation*, London: Hutchinson Education.

Glynn, M. (2014) *Black Men, Invisibility and Crime*, Abingdon & New York: Routledge.

Greig, J. (1932) *The Letters of David Hume*, Oxford: Clarendon Press.

Gunter, A. (2010) *Growing up Bad: Black Youth, Road Culture & Badness in an East London Neighbourhood*, London: The Tufnell Press.

Herrnstein, R. J. & Murray, C. (1994) *The Bell Curve: Intelligence and Class Structure in American Life*, New York & London: Free Press.

HMSO (1824) Vagrancy Act. An Act for the Punishment of idle and disorderly Persons, and Rogues and Vagabonds, in that Part of Great Britain called England. London.

HMSO (1968) The Race Relations Act. An Act to make fresh provision with respect to discrimination on racial grounds, and to make provision with respect to relations between people of different racial origins. Chapter 71. London.

Hobbs, D. (1988) *Doing the Business*, Oxford: Oxford University Press.

Hobbs, D. (2013) *Lush Life: Constructing Organized Crime in the UK*, Oxford: Oxford University Press.

Isaac, B. (2001) *The Invention of Racism in Classical Antiquity*, Princeton: Princeton University Press.

Jagessar, M. (2007) *Black Theory in Britain: A Reader*, London: Equinox.

Kant, I. (1997) 'Immanuel Kant: On the Different Races of Man. Immanuel Kant: Of National Characteristics. Immanuel Kant: Physical Geography', in Eze, C. (ed.), *Race and the Enlightenment: A Reader*, Oxford: Blackwell, pp. 38–64.

Lea, J. (2002) *Crime and Modernity*, London: Sage.

Lea, J. & Young, J. (1984) *What Is to Be Done about Law and Order?* Harmondsworth: Penguin.

Lipsky, M. & Olsen, D. (1977) *Commission Politics: The Processing of Racial Crisis in America*, New Brunswick: Transaction Books.

Mayhew, H. (1969) *London Labour and the London Poor*, London: Dover Publications.

Monrose, K. (2016) 'Struggling, Juggling and Street Corner Hustling: The Street Economy of Newham's Black Community', in Antonopoulos, G. (ed.), *Illegal Entrepreneurship, Organized Crime and Social Control, Essays in Honor of Professor Dick Hobbs*, Geneva: Springer, pp. 73–84.

Monrose, K. (2017) 'Shame, Scandal and Respectability Amongst the Children of *Windrush* Generation: A Scholarly Omission', in Hobbs, D. (ed.), *Mischief, Morality and Mobs, Essays in Honour of Geoffrey Pearson*, New York & Abingdon: Routledge, pp. 59–82.

Morton, J. (2000) *East End Gangland*, London: Time Warner.

Newburn, T. (1990) *Crime & Criminal Justice Policy*, London: Longman.

Newham Monitoring Project (1991) *Forging a Black Community: Asian and Afro Caribbean Struggles in Newham*, London: NMP/CARF.

Noble, M. (1984) *Jamaica Airman: A Black Airman in Britain, 1943 and After*, London: New Beacon Books.

O'Neil, G. (2000) *My East End: Memories of Life in Cockney London*, London: Penguin.

Phillips, M. & Phillips, T. (1998) *Windrush: The Irresistible Rise of Multi-Racial Britain*, London: Harper Collins.

Pryce, K. (1979) *Endless Pressure*, Bristol: Bristol Classical Press.

Rodney, W. (1973) *How Europe Underdeveloped Africa*, London: Bogle–L'Ouverture Publications.

Rose, J. (1992) *A Climate of Fear: The Murder of PC Blakelock and the Case of the Tottenham Three*, Bloomsbury: Sale.

Scarman, L. (1981) *The Scarman Report*, London: Home Office.

Scarman, L. (1986) *The Scarman Report (Revised edn)*, Harmondsworth: Penguin.

Scobie, E. (1972) *Black Britannia: A History of Blacks in Britain*, Chicago: Johnson Publishing Company.

Selvon, S. (1967) *The Lonely Londoners*, London: Penguin.

Selvon, S. (1975) *Moses Ascending*, London: Penguin.

Sherwood, M. (1985) *Many Struggles – West Indian Workers & Service Personnel in Britain (1939–1945)*, London: Karia Press.

Smart, C. (1995) *Law, Crime and Sexuality: Essays in Feminism*, London: Sage.

Solomos, J. (1988) *Black Youth, Racism and the State: The Politics of Ideology and Policy*, Cambridge: Cambridge University Press.

Staples, R. (1976) *An Introduction to Black Sociology*, San Francisco: McGraw-Hill.

Thatcher, M. (1978) *World in Action*, Season 14, Episode 11, broadcast 20.30, 30 January, Granada Television.

Williams, E. (1944) *Capitalism and Slavery*, Chapel Hill: University of North Carolina.

Winder, R. (2013) *Bloody Foreigners: The Story of Immigration to Britain*, London: Abacus.

Winston, G. T. (1901) 'The Relations of the Whites and the Negroes', *Annual of the American Academy of Politics and Social Science*, 17: 108–109.

Chapter 3

Research approach and methods

This chapter will provide an account of the methodological processes under-taken for carrying out this ethnography. To start with, I will present the profiles of the main participants within the study. I will follow by outlining the key aims and objectives of the project, and the manner in which it evolved. Next I will bring attention to the primary strategy used within the research process, namely thematic ethnographic interviews, and speak on both the advantages and disadvantages of such an approach. Topics such as sampling, linguistic codes, access and validity will also be discussed.

Seeing voices: a portrait of the respondents

Blacker

Blacker was born and raised in East London to Jamaican parents who arrived in Britain during the 1950s. Open, calm and methodical, Blacker described his life in great detail. The home in which Blacker was brought up was unremark-able and stable. His parents met and married whilst in Jamaica. His father migrated to Britain in the 1950s and after a short spell sent for his wife to come over and join him. At school Blacker considered himself academically able, and possessed a healthy interest in sports, particularly athletics and foot-ball. As a youth, Blacker had an inquisitive mind but he found secondary school frustrating at times, especially when teachers failed to address his ques-tions and curiosity. As a result, he felt that he was marked out as a disruptive influence upon other pupils.

Over time, this led him to being excluded from school on a number of occa-sions – eleven in all. By the age of fourteen Blacker was permanently expelled from the educational system, and spent the rest of his formative years on the streets, inevitably drifting into crime. His criminal activity started with low-level theft, such as stealing car radios and bicycles, but this soon escalated to burglaries. This pattern continued for a number of years until his arrest and subsequent incarceration. Blacker deeply regretted being sentenced to prison, and seeing the devastating effect it had on his parents. However, over time he became a recidivist, by selling drugs whilst feeding a newly acquired drug habit. Blacker openly states that he did well from crime, and made a lot of money. He claims that, because of his attitude, had he grown up in the Caribbean, he would have been dead by now. Blacker cites two reasons for his cessation of criminality: fatherhood, and an attempt to rob him of his life in a firearm-related incident.

Blue

Born and raised in East London, Blue is a qualified tradesman, having served an apprenticeship upon leaving school. Blue thrived in what he considered a 'normal' upbringing, and enjoyed school immensely. He states that his upbringing was typified by living within a community that was peaceful and harmonious. He recalls all races and cultures getting on famously, and felt sheltered from the racism that ravaged the part of London in which he was located. This said, the turning point in his life was what he describes as his first real, impactful experience of racism. This episode and its consequences led to Blue dropping out of full-time employment, and questioning matters he had previously taken for granted. He disowned his religious upbringing of Catholicism and instead chose to embrace the lifestyle of Rastafari.

Blue has experienced a turbulent relationship with enforcement agencies and has a record of arrest. He is unrepentant towards his past actions with regard to the police, and is explicit that given the opportunity, he will resort to violence (which he describes as defence) to defeat 'Babylon' or racism. His is a story of an individual whom racial discrimination forced to become a self-defined anti-hero, or a man who, in his own words, says the authorities 'shouldn't fuck with'.

Burglar

Burglar is loud and gregarious and of commanding stature. After his size and presence, the most noticeable thing about Burglar is the way he speaks. He effortlessly moves from speaking in a coarse East End cockney accent – even dipping into rhyming slang on occasions – to a broad Jamaican brogue. Burglar is well respected and well known, but has a fearful reputation as a serious individual. He is a self-defined 'council estate kid' who grew up living on the eleventh floor of a high rise in Canning Town, where he attended school. He describes his life as unremarkable, since his experiences are the same as those of many people he grew up around. Despite being a father of five, Burglar lives alone outside of London. He states that he no longer has anything to do with the East End if he can help it, but was nonetheless very interested in sharing his experiences of time spent there.

He speaks of his first girlfriend, who 'wasn't allowed to have black boyfriends' so kept him hidden. When he did make the short journey to the suburbs to meet her, he noticed how clean the streets were and how the homes were well kept, and vowed one day to live in a place like that. Police harassment was a daily occurrence for young men from the part of Newham where he lived, and he was regularly arrested for 'being in the wrong place, at the wrong time, with the wrong people'.

Burglar confesses to being a womaniser, and has no qualms in describing them in derogatory terms. He suggests that white women should be used and abused at every opportunity, be it sexually or materially, as he sees them as doing the same to black men; but he seems to direct most of his anger towards black women, whom he regards as 'leeches and parasites'. Offensive and emotionally driven as our exchanges were, Burglar is forthright and unapologetic for his opinions, which will make uncomfortable reading for some.

Gilly

British-born Gilly defines himself as a 'bad boy turned good'. Clearly an engaging and articulate individual, he is the youngest of those formally interviewed, being in his early thirties. He currently lives and works in central London. He describes his upbringing in Newham as comfortable, and devoid of any major 'drama'. His parents were married in St Lucia and came to Britain in the 1960s. Like many others from the Eastern Caribbean, he was brought up a Roman Catholic and attended church regularly. He aspired one day to become a professional footballer, but a complicated injury meant that his dream was unfulfilled. Subsequent lack of direction and idleness saw him drift into a street gang occupied with criminal activity. After witnessing several of his peers receive long prison sentences, he decided to strategise an exit from the gang. He enrolled in further education and then higher education, where he eventually obtained an MBA from a prestigious establishment. He explains in great detail his experiences as a working-class black male in what he perceives to be as a white-middle-class-dominated world. He states quite openly that one of the best things about going to university was that it provided fertile ground for him to recommence his drug dealing activities as a means of meeting his tuition fees. He suggests that his enterprise of drug distribution on the university campuses he attended proved to be more lucrative, profitable and safe than the time spent in the gang and on the streets.

Greenie

Greenie was born and raised in East London and was raised single-handedly by his mother. He speaks with great fondness of her, acknowledging the struggles and hardships she endured to provide for him. He describes in detail the privation he felt as a fatherless black child in Thatcherite Britain. Greenie emotionally reflected on his adolescence, when he noticed the differences between white households and black households. He saw black homes, including his own, as disruptive, chaotic and confused, whereas white homes seemed stable, peaceful and ordered. This had an impact on his relationship choices, as he refuses to date black women, who he feels have very little to offer him. Greenie freely admits that there have been occasions when he has hated being black and wished that he was white, because a white life looked easier.

Due to the strong personalities and larger-than-life characters that sur-rounded him in Newham, Greenie found it difficult at times to fit in, and strove to leave East London as soon as he could, viewing it as an environment that stifled his personal growth. His is a story charged with emotional highs and lows, and chronicles the journey of a fatherless black male trying to make sense of his own existence.

Fat Larry

Fat Larry was born in Berkshire to Barbadian parents, who shortly after his birth relocated to East London. His mother was a factory worker, whilst his father worked in a steel foundry. He attended school in Newham, and was actively involved with the local church community as both a choir boy and an altar boy. As a youth he held early aspirations of being an athlete, but this ambition evolved into a quest to join the British Army by being a member of the Cadets. This goal was soon dashed, however, as his parents refused to give him the necessary consent to enlist.

Fat Larry speaks candidly of the ever-present violence that surrounded him, both at home and in school. In graphic terms, he also describes the culture of racism in school, and the acts of violence that were meted out to teachers or anybody else whom he perceived as being disrespectful towards him. He saw violence in the home as igniting the fuse of rebellion within him, and causing the resulting drift into crime. Shortly after leaving school he became a car thief, a burglar and finally an armed robber. He attributes to good fortune alone his escape from serving a lengthy prison sentence, and has decided to quit 'whilst ahead'.

Fire

Fire is a self-defined 'roadman'. He is fifty-five years old and was born on the Caribbean island of St Kitts. Fire is talkative and energetic, and enthusiastic-ally engaged with the research process. He was one of the few respondents to arrive in Britain with both of his parents. He doesn't recall much of St Kitts other than the sounds, particularly the call of the crickets, croaking lizards and tree frogs at dusk. Fire first became aware of discrimination at an early age, when he noted the obvious differences between the treatment of his white classmates and that of children of another race.

Fire is keen to mention that he is a typical East Ender and has mastered the art of 'making a grand out of a oner' (transforming £100 into £1,000). Fire is particularly vocal on issues that surround the configuration of the West Indian family unit in Britain, and is refreshingly judgemental on muted topics such as domestic corporal punishment and inter-generational conflict. Fire, although a proud Kittitian, is passionate about and fiercely protective of his British and East London status. He is concerned, however, about how West Indian culture in Britain has been diluted and slowly eroded, toward what he sees as the catastrophic consequences of this for black West Indian youth. Fire has a great sense of humour and offered some acute insight into black life in Newham during the 1970s and 1980s, and the profound impact that these experiences have had on shaping his life.

Mr Brown

Mr Brown was one of the oldest of my formally interviewed informants. He is imposing in stature, but possesses a kind, soft and gentle demeanour. Mr Brown has acted as head bouncer for a number of well-known nightclubs in London. Working in this industry means he is easy to engage with and communicates well. I found Mr Brown to be open and willing to reflect on his life in great detail, particularly in regard to his upbringing in the Caribbean. He is a proud West Indian, and intends to return and live permanently in the land of his birth. He was one of the few formal respondents who migrated to England by boat, and has lucid memories of the long trip across the Atlantic Ocean. Unlike others who came to England during the 1970s, he was not located within an established black community, but a majority white community in rural Essex. This led to his being involved in daily fistfights, since he was the only black person in the school he attended. Mr Brown clearly understood the potency of racism, but as an individual who has had many years' experience of dealing with people, now chooses to react to it in a measured, non-confrontational manner. His is a story of a man who was free and uninhibited in the West Indies, but felt imprisoned and confined in Britain.

Mr Gold

Mr Gold is a married grandfather born in St Lucia. His parents migrated to England when he was two years old, leaving him in the care of extended family members. He speaks proudly of his humble beginnings in St Lucia, and tackles head-on the issues faced by the children left behind by migrating parents. He arrived in Britain in the early 1970s aged thirteen, and describes in great detail the emotional void that existed between him and his parents because of their migration, and the consequences of this.

Mr Gold's story, like those of many of the respondents who were born in the West Indies but spent the majority of their lives in Britain, highlights a crisis of identity and a quest for belonging. He provides the reader with a privileged insight into a realm of black British culture that is often hidden.

Nev

Nev is a civil servant born to Jamaican parents. Nev was raised as a Jehovah's Witness, which has assisted in shaping many of the beliefs that he still holds today. His story is marked by the consequences of being excommunicated and dis-fellowshipped by the Jehovah's Witness community in his late teens, which led to him being shunned by his family and friends for a number of years. Like others in the study, he considered himself skilled at sports, and stated that whilst at school he was considered the 'star boy' in cricket, football and rugby. However, his performances on the sports field were hindered by religious restrictions and obligations placed upon him.

He eventually plans to return to the church, and claims that his faith has not strayed too far away from him. His views regarding marriage and children are firm, and bound by biblical doctrine. He refuses to father children outside wedlock, and is an advocate of administering strict forms of discipline to children, to ensure that they obey both the law of the Bible and the law of the land. Although he has visited Jamaica many times and owns property there, Nev aspires to live in the USA – a place where he believes a 'black man can really make it'.

Pretty

Pretty is a corporate executive within the financial sector. He is unmarried, and has no children. Materially, Pretty has done very well, and enjoys all the trappings associated with a six-figure salary. He now lives in an exclusive London postcode. Although he was born in East London, as a teen Pretty and his parents relocated to Jamaica, where he was forced to undertake an additional year of education in order to be up to speed with the Caribbean standards of schooling. This was surprise to him as he believed that the English standard of education was considerably more advanced than that of the West Indies. On his return to England in his late teens, he was appalled at the lack of discipline and aspiration among black Britons of his age. Pretty firmly believes that blacks in Britain need to be shaken up in order to be successful within the framework of British society. He defines himself as 'politically homeless but politically aware', and grounds his views in 'reality not idealism'. He is extremely protective of the plight of black women in Britain, and suggests that to date someone outside his race is, for him, unproductive and serves no lasting purpose in dealing with the struggles faced by black men.

Red

Red is in his sixties. He's a married father of two who has been in Britain since the age of nine after arriving from Antigua. With pride and passion, Red speaks of Caribbean life, and the high moral standards and supportive nature of the family and community he was raised in. Red provides an in-depth insight into the reality of a Caribbean upbringing, as well as a detailed account of the cultural transitions experienced in moving from Antigua to England. Red speaks of the residue of post-colonialism in Antigua, particularly in reference to employment and career pathways. He identifies shadism as one of the main obstacles for individual progress on the island. The psychological complexities associated with black cultural identity for the post-*Windrush* generation are a subject that Red speaks on with authority, informed by his own lived experience.

Soldier

The first thing you will notice about Soldier is his manner of dress. His attire is immaculate and impressive. Soldier is in his late fifties and was born in South East London. He is single and without children. At a young age he moved to Newham, where his lived with his parents and two older siblings. Soldier remarked that music was of primary importance in the home whilst growing up. His father owned a sound system, and was well known for running popular blues dances and shubeens around London during the 1970s and 1980s. Soldier took notice of this and shortly after leaving school began promoting and staging music events. In time his prowess for promotion developed, and his company enjoyed a great level of success. As a result, Soldier left East London and enjoyed living a lucrative lifestyle in various cities throughout the UK. He counted a number of well-known celebrities and luminaries as both close friends and associates. He states that procuring wealth and status was easy, but holding onto it is what proved to be difficult. A jet-set lifestyle meant that cocaine quickly became part of the picture, and involvement with cocaine, and then crack, proved to be his downfall. His addiction brought out a side of his personality that he wasn't aware existed. As his resources began to dwindle because of his habit, he began to off-load his belongings to satisfy his craving for crack, until nothing was left. Soldier confessed that at one stage he lived in a crack house. His story is one of a rollercoaster, on which he has experienced the heights of wealth and the depths of drug abuse.

Informal exchanges

Cletus

A retired car worker from Trinidad who came to Britain in the 1950s and still lives in East London, vowing never to return to the West Indies.

Faro

A retired unskilled worker now relocated to St Lucia after living in Britain for thirty-five years. His mother died when he was a child and he was raised by his grandmother. Faro had no formal education as such. As a small boy he worked the land in rural St Lucia. He travelled to Curaçao for a period and worked in a cane field hewing bamboo and sugar cane, but this was short-lived, and he returned to St Lucia and was employed within the public works division. He migrated to Britain in 1962 and settled in East London. He planned to spend only five years there, so never took the step of purchasing a home. His first job was as a pipefitter's mate and he vividly recalls how bitter the 1963 winter was in London. Faro then worked as a cleaning operative for British Telecommunications for a number of years before retiring in 1992. He returned to St Lucia a year later. He reflects upon the protracted period spent in Britain as something he had to do, and mentions that the only things he misses about London are horse racing, betting shops and going to the pub.

Former primary school teacher

A retired white male from East London who has many years' teaching experience in various areas in London and the Home Counties. He was a primary school teacher in Newham during the 1980s, when he had first-hand experience of witnessing the difficulties that black children faced at school, on the streets and within the home. Because of this insight he was one of the few white teachers who were able to engage, discipline and encourage the black male students he taught effectively, and was able to tailor and establish successful rules for conduct within his own teaching practice. A youth football team he ran in central Newham drew in participants from all over the borough, and proved to be an enriching experience for these youngsters, since, once they were immersed in football, matters of race were, albeit momentarily, cast aside.

Hubert

A St Lucian who is now retired and lives in Newham. A painter and decorator by trade, Hubert, like Cletus, has decided to spend his retirement years in Britain, where he arrived in the 1950s. Despite his advanced years, Hubert still visits the West Indies but is adamant that he would not return to the Island permanently. He is a proud West Indian and has high regard for West Indian codes and conduct, particularly in regard to propriety and respectability.

Millie

A middle-aged married mother born to Jamaican parents. Born and raised in Huddersfield, West Yorkshire, she now lives and practices law in London.

Miss Marie

Miss Marie is a beautifully soft-spoken mother of four, a grandmother and a great-grandmother. She is in her nineties and resides in the Caribbean after spending thirty-three years in Britain.

Miss Marie was raised in an agricultural community in St Lucia. Her mother died when she was nine, so she was compelled to look after her younger siblings. Her father was a farmer, who, she said, 'worked so hard to provide for all of his children.' She openly states that father loved her very much, and how proud of him she is and that she misses him deeply. As a girl Miss Marie enjoyed learning and recalls eagerly walking to school barefooted, so as not to get her school shoes dirty. Despite her age she still remembers the assortment of plants and flowers that adorned her route to class, and described their properties to me in detail.

She obtained her first job as a store girl when she was nineteen, after leaving her country home for the town. She was married in 1961, and migrated to Britain in 1962 to join her husband, leaving three children behind. Upon arrival in Britain she lived in Plaistow, Canning Town and East Ham before settling in Forest Gate for twenty-three years. She worked as a seamstress, and in various factories, such as Cable's, Ever Ready and Lesney's, the Matchbox Toy manufacturers. Her final job was as a cleaning operative for British Rail. Almost instantly upon retirement, she returned to the West Indies.

Miss Marie was raised as a Seventh Day Adventist, but left the church in her youth. However, she has recently become baptised into it again. The church always played a key part of her life, and had an important role in the way in which she has raised her children. As a female member of the *Windrush* generation, she provides us with a number of valuable insights.

Jughead

Jughead was one of three homeless black men whom I engaged with while they danced and hawked plastic flowers and single cigarettes outside the world-famous Bobby's Happy House record store on 125th Street in Harlem, New York City. A sunny autumnal Saturday afternoon found Jughead and his companions dancing around a single woofer speaker placed on the sidewalk outside the store. A few passersby nonchalantly threw coins in a box while Jughead and his crew swayed and jived to the Southern soul and blues sounds being played. As a visitor, I was intrigued and taken by their skilled and effortless display.

Jughead acted as the spokesperson of the dance trio and, impressed by my English accent, referred to me as 'Professor Marley', because of my academic ambitions and my long dreadlocks. He was happy to speak to me, despite his colleagues saying I was interrupting their hustle. Jughead was full of judgment and controversy, and made it clear that he objected to having any biological links with West Indians or Africans, whom he openly defined in derogatory terms. He stood fast to being acknowledged as American, not as African-American. In his opinion American and European slave traders were only doing to the Africans what the Africans were doing to each other. In fact, he suggests that the Europeans learnt slavery from the Africans. Jughead was good company and the hours spent listening to him were undoubtedly time well spent.

Rambo

Rambo grew up in a poor rural community in Jamaica with his grandparents. He has been living in Britain since the 1990s. He is vocal about his upbringing in the West Indies and provides us with an undiluted and harrowing account of the corporal punishment he received.

Terry, Phil and Peter the bookie

Three white males in their sixties. A tradesman, a London taxi driver and a betting shop worker. All these men were born and raised in Newham, and now live in South Essex. They provided me with a white working-class perspective on black presence in Britain. They relayed an insight to me that, by virtue of being a black man, I would not ordinarily be party to.

Objectives and aims

This ethnography, although largely drawn from a successfully completed PhD thesis, had its genesis as a postgraduate degree dissertation that examined factors related to gun culture within black British communities. My aim at the time was to gauge the level of concern within black communities regarding reports in the news media of so-called 'black on black' gun crime, and claims that the streets of Britain were awash with black males liberally discharging firearms on a daily basis (Walsh, 2003; McLagan, 2006). As a member of a black community in London, I was curious to confirm the accuracy of such assertions. I began my investigation by conducting extensive backyard research, and spoke to my numerous associates and friends within various black communities across Britain, to consider their opinions about gun culture. The reaction I found was unlike the sensationalised themes depicted in the media. Yes, I encountered individuals who claimed to possess and carry firearms casually, but they were few and far between, a fact validated by Metropolitan Police figures assembled from initiatives and directives such as Operations Trident[1] and Trafalgar,[2] and figures obtained from the Greater Manchester police.

There is no doubt that a firearm-related incident and the effects it produces are both lasting and devastating, but in statistical terms, compared to the extent of other forms of interpersonal violence and weapon-enabled crime, gun-related incidents were insignificant. For example, figures for the period of my graduate study showed that both recorded and reported firearm-related incidents measured fewer than 1 per cent (Home Office Recorded Crime Dataset, 2003).

Amplification of black criminality came as no real surprise, as the demonisation of black communities has been a constant fixture within the British media for decades (Hall, 1973; McRobbie & Thornton, 2009). Let us not forget that during the 1970s the black male was commonly seen as anti-establishment and rebellious, in the 1980s he was held responsible for 'mugging' or street robbery, and during the 1990s and beyond he was considered an armed urban terrorist. For me, gun violence and the 'emerging' gun culture was a matter of old wine in new bottles, given the lengthy and but often silent history of gun culture in Britain going back to at least the eighteenth century (Lee Malcolm, 2004).

Up to this point, the research I conducted disproved many of the myths propagated about the emergence of gun culture within black communities across Britain. The stale, regurgitated guesswork that attributed violence to poor educational achievement and absent father paradigms negated the systematic failures in the provision of schooling for black students and those considered working-class. My research noticed that the majority of men implicated in this form of criminality did not live on sink estates, nor were from broken homes. Many came from normal nuclear family configurations, with employed parents, in owner-occupied dwellings. As a result, and as is true with a number of research projects, I arrived at a conclusion that left me with many more questions than I began with.

Punch (1996) suggests that political issues often have an impact on research within criminology/sociology, and I quickly found this to be true. Prior to the commencement of my research, reported gun-related incidents had dramatically increased. The government, in response, imposed harsher sentences for firearm possession (1968 Section 5 Firearm Act amendment (b) January 2004),[3,4] and enforcement agencies adopted ever more proactive tactics in an attempt to curb this escalation. This of course was commendable insofar as it stemmed the tide of potential bloodshed, but it proved to be a disaster for my research intentions, as access to respondents suddenly dried up. Nonetheless, I decided that the research had to carry on.

Because of the already sensitive and high-risk nature of the study, there were new logistical barriers that I was now forced to negotiate. Until then, both offenders and victims of gun crime had been willing to speak to me informally, and quite candidly, but now I encountered a wall of silence. I negotiated this by making myself available to attend public forums and community meetings in order to obtain an alternative source of sentiments on gun crime, as well as utilising these opportunities to network, and develop links, with interested parties whom I could later call upon. However, I found many of these forums became (understandably at times) emotionally led, which led the matter to be dealt with simplistically, and were neither empirical nor scientific in terms of offering a valuable assessment that would assist in producing an original contribution to knowledge on gun culture.

However, I began to detect that, although undeniably there were a very small number of men who participated in criminal activity, as a rule the majority of black men in Britain strove to live within the margins of the law and embrace criminal preclusion. Those within this majority, I concluded, are not often spoken about, and I reasoned that an original and interesting angle of sociological investigation would be to look at the true-life stories and narratives of black men here in Britain. This would be a move away from speaking about them simply in terms of their relationship with criminal justice and enforcement. As an academic in training, I tied this enquiry to my existing curiosity about black cultural identity and representation.

The importance of narratives

> The human being is always a teller of stories, he lives surrounded by his own stories and those of other people, he sees everything that happens to him in terms of stories, and he tries to live his life as if he was recounting it.
>
> (Bruner, 1987:21)

Narratives and personal stories are the manner in which we as human beings alleviate the existential vacuums, and feelings of life's meaninglessness, that we all experience at some point. Our past and present are constantly constructed, deconstructed and reconstructed, in order that a cognitive schema of our life's theme may be formulated. This never ceases, as our personal stories and accounts of events enable us to make sense of both positive and negative experiences. Moreover, narratives highlight the very practical applications that oral testaments bring to social science, by bridging the divide between people, and encouraging new and alternative understandings of chaotic and complex concepts such as identities and gender. By learning, and cultivating the art of listening, the ethnographer gains a greater insight into the innermost regions of their respondents' lives.

These are factors I held at the forefront of my mind while in the field. My main objective was to unearth the hidden experiences, narratives and life stories of the post-*Windrush* generation, a generation that until now has been neglected by academic enquiry, and I saw an ethnographic approach as the most suitable. I considered an interpretive approach significantly more sufficient than other methods, as it would provide a broader understanding of the life course of the men under discussion than would a methodology wholly reliant upon statistical information. My approach would provide a robust portrait of their lives and offer commentary that would inevitably translate into a repository of rich dependable data:

> Every culture has a world view, an orientation, which defines and orders reality, and the ethnographer seeks to present a description of human behaviour which reflects the universe of the 'native.' He seeks to describe and explicate the value system of the group under study.
>
> (Soloway & Walters, 1977:160)

For me, the most appealing and satisfying technique of ethnographic investigation was to place myself amongst people and promiscuously use my senses to listen, see and feel, in an attempt to make sense of both verbal and non-verbal communication – to be a social voyeur, if you will. In fact, I, like many, am taken to 'people watching' and putting my sociological eye to work, so I was enthused at the prospect of delving into uncharted cerebral waters to reveal serviceable data. I fully intended to utilise every privileged phase of the research process, and arrive at a point that inspired me to metaphorically roll my sleeves up, get out there and be prepared to get my hands dirty.

Black by black research

A few noteworthy studies related to black life in Britain have been compiled by those who exist outside the black British cultural experience. I am in no doubt that the research endeavours of these scholars are rigorous, but it remains my opinion that the true essence of the internal functions of black community membership is perhaps better presented by a member of the subject group, because, theoretically speaking, an affinity between researcher and informant is more likely to yield more reliable data:

> I'm glad to see another black face flexing and investigating other black faces, because these privileged white researchers like to try to walk in our shoes, but remember, they can take our shoes off whenever they want. We have to walk in those shoes all the time. So it's good to see and speak to someone who is going to understand what you're talking about, without getting it twisted when it's put out there.
>
> (Gilly)

Gilly makes valid points. One cannot grasp a full appreciation of a phenomenon by osmosis, or by being a sightseer or tourist, as Stein (2006) also suggests. For the ethnographer to understand the mechanisms that lie at the heart of an issue, he/she has to fully immerse themselves into that community (Anderson, 1976, 1999; Pryce, 1979; Hobbs, 1988). It therefore becomes essential for the researcher to be part of, and, where possible, 'break bread with', the subject group on their terms, in order to obtain an intimate insight into their culture.

In the field

> Fieldwork, at its core, is a long social process of coming to terms with culture. It is a process that begins before one enters the field and continues long after one leaves it.
>
> (Van Maanen, 1988)

The study was based in Newham in East London, and consisted of both informal and formal exchanges. Formal exchanges took the form of thematic interviews, designed to elicit respondents' perceptions of the various life issues facing black men in Britain. The interview design, although rigid in terms of the topics tackled, had the added attraction of being open-ended, so that any emergent themes could be drawn upon and discussed (Brewer, 2000; McNeil & Chapman, 2005). As stated, my objective was to allow respondents to 'paint a picture' of their lives. However, one of my primary concerns involved a possible shift of emphasis from my original research intentions:

> The first few days or even weeks of a study may bring in only superficial information, along with bits of data that do not seem to make sense or do not fit together. One, who has become accustomed to measuring progress in terms of pages read or written, naturally finds this beginning stage frustrating. Unless obviously dramatic [things] are unfolding before our eyes, it may seem that nothing is happening.
>
> (Whyte, 1984:69)

These fears were met in my very first interview, which auspiciously produced some results I had not bargained for, and these, over time, became extremely useful. Issues that I had not given thought to beforehand, and were not included within my interview design, were broached; and, instead of throwing me off course, as I anticipated they would, such responses provided me with some very rich and original data.

Informal exchanges took place during conversations with individuals I met in various locations, such as day centres, hospitals or eateries, or simply by spending time on the street. In reality the research site was all around me, at all times, by virtue of my being an outsider-insider, as it were. Even within the more challenging times of my personal life, such as being a dialysis patient, I found that my conversations with other West Indian patients and health practitioners steered towards obtaining usable data. For example, I occasionally spoke with superannuated *Windrush* arrivals (who are now unfortunately deceased but whose comments are included) on topics relevant to the project. I often found informal exchanges to be valuable because the responses acted as a way of validating the information obtained from my primary subjects. In addition, it was within these informal exchanges that new ideas and potential avenues for further investigation arose, and piqued my interest all the more.

I made it a priority to keep a notebook in my possession at all times, or to be near a telephone (many reasoning sessions took place on the phone), in order that memos could be taken, as these reasoning's, which could last hours, were not recorded. It was often the smaller points of fact hidden in the stream of gathered information that turned out to be gems of data, which is where my trusted thought diary became an unparalleled resource. Keeping a thought diary for me was not an easy task, as it required an unconventional form of discipline that differed from keeping a notebook. Continuity and consistency in inputting both lucid and sometimes unintelligible contemplations into what became a well-worn and threadbare jotter made for a laborious chore. However, the labour was handsomely rewarded as the diary proved to be a valuable asset.

I refused to conduct formal interviews within an informal setting such as a night club, social club or pub/bar, as I knew from previous research experience that the results would be less than favourable, because of noise and other distractions. Formal exchanges took place under strict conditions, where the respondent had been previously briefed, and made aware of my research intentions, and told that the occasions we spent together would, with their consent, be audio-recorded. Moreover, throughout the process of the fieldwork it was important that I kept sober and cognisant at all times, particularly as I was aware just how close I was to some of the respondents. As I have stated, sharing what I considered to be a similar worldview seemed, at the outset, to make my research task increasingly doable. However, the main problem with such proximity, one that I had not accounted for, and I will go on to discuss later, was my ability to produce a work that was value-free, objective and reflexive (Van Maanen, 1988; Hesse-Biber, 2006).

Sampling frame

My sampling frame was reliant on chain referral sampling (or snowballing), drawn from a varying population that was then divided into two groups. The primary sample group included the formal thematic interviews of ten men. The second group included a larger group of approximately thirty individuals who were interviewed informally and, as stated above, in a less structured fashion. Researchers are often reminded that our sampling frames/choices are in some way flawed, and cannot be fully relied upon just because of their size. A common criticism is that the chosen sample is not large enough to represent the whole population. Moreover, some may also suggest that sample size may limit scientific research, because one cannot apply all the professed knowledge of a subject to a few examples (Silverman, 2000; Mason, 2002). Nevertheless, the ethnographer must insist that, although the sample may be smaller than the actual size of the population it denotes, its representation is both pragmatic and demonstrable: part of a population, organisation or system we have studied to represent meaningfully the whole from which it was drawn (Becker, 1998:67).

I therefore drew my formal sample group from a varying population of West Indian men, with age being my only concern (typically thirty-five to fifty-five). Contact with some participants was primarily established through personal acquaintances (Wright & Decker, 1994). This avoided the problem of the pervasive mistrust of strangers that is often evident within West Indian public life (Gunst, 2004). Requesting consent to conduct an interview was relatively straightforward, and most of those whom I approached seemed enthusiastic to contribute. However, some logistical difficulties arose after an initial interview date had been scheduled. For example, some failed to arrive at our pre-arranged meet-up, and others suddenly disappeared and were no longer contactable. This I found hugely frustrating. I often questioned myself, and at times felt that their absence and tardiness may have been due to my failure to clearly and adequately outline the intentions of the research. Consequently, I revised my approach. I decided to provide respondents with a more detailed outline of the project, inclusive of aims and objectives, and a few paragraphs to promote a better understanding of what the interview procedure entailed. Further to this, I gave out business cards in an attempt to project myself in a more professional manner, in order to show my commitment to the study. Hobbs points out:

> On commencing the research, I was keen to enter a field, that is, to be a *real* academic with a clipboard, a firm notion of what I was about, and a self confidence that would no doubt emanate from my newly acquired status.
>
> (Hobbs, in Hobbs & May, 1993:47)

I also made sure that I provided documented evidence declaring that the interview would be both anonymous and conducted within the ethical boundaries of the British Sociological Association. This, I felt, would put the participant at ease, and help develop a more psychologically secure exchange:

> Sociologists have a responsibility to ensure that the physical, social and psychological well-being of research participants is not adversely affected by the research. They should strive to protect the rights of those they study, their interests, sensitivities and privacy, while recognising the difficulty of balancing potentially conflicting interests.
>
> (Statement of Ethical Practice for the British Sociological Association, March 2002:13)

Upon the completion of an interview, within the debriefing process, I asked the participant to pass my details on to others who they felt would like to participate, and might have something of value to offer the study. This proved effective, and towards the end of my data collection I was in receipt of copious text messages, e-mails and voicemails from individuals who either wanted to partake or knew of someone who wanted to.

At this point it is important that I speak on how participants are defined in this text. I am fully aware of the interchangeability of terms such as 'respondent', 'subject' and 'informant' within academic writing, but it is the last term, 'informant', that I need to draw attention to. As is true with most minority and sub cultural groups, members of black communities are often suspicious of those who attempt to investigate and probe into their lives. Therefore, linguistic codes that are commonly used by social scientists to describe those interviewed (whether formally or informally) need to be carefully calculated and accounted for. For example, the term 'informant' carries a highly significant connotation when it is levelled at individuals within some black communities. Gunst (2004), in her work on Jamaican gangs, qualifies this, and mentions that by directing the term 'informant' (or 'informer') at an interviewee, regardless of the context in which it is framed, is akin to handing out a death sentence, as it is automatically assumed that an informant is one who works in collusion with enforcement agencies. This of course was not the case in this project; nonetheless it is incredibly important that liberal use of this term was restricted, and instead the terms 'respondent' or 'participant' selected.

The interview process

> Most methods textbooks treat interviewing as a conversation between two people – the interviewer and the interviewee. The interviewer asks questions and the interviewee responds to them. But if you think about it, this is a peculiar kind of conversation. In an interview one person – the interviewee – reveals information about him or herself; the other does not. One person – the interviewer – directs the conversation often with expectations for what should happen during that conversation, and for what constitutes a 'correct' answer; the other does not. One person – the interviewer – decides when the questions have been satisfactorily answered, and closes the conversation; the other does not. In this sense, an interview is an odd type of conversation indeed. In what other kind of conversation is there such a lopsided exchange?
>
> (Esterberg, 2002:84)

As stated earlier, one of the advantages of culturally being a part of the group which one is researching, or 'going native', is in respect of language. An appreciation of the linguistic code, accent and colloquialisms of respondent's aids understanding of the data offered, and it is of course the data that is the infrastructure upon which any ethnography stands. Therefore the researcher has to develop a dual juggling form of strategy within the interview process, wherein the spoken language is culturally inclusive but at the same time the written language is academically sound: I was in effect, exploring two cultures: one working class, my native culture; the other academic, to which I aspired (Hobbs, in Hobbs & May, 1993:51).

Space was an important factor to consider within the interview process, as this determined whether the respondent felt comfortable enough to speak freely. As it was at the forefront of my mind to allow the interviewee to feel at ease, I insisted that formal interviews be conducted, if at all possible, in a location where they were comfortable. Thankfully many agreed to this. As has been pointed out, a written document outlining the main objectives of the study was provided. This we read over again together, allowing any questions regarding the interview to be raised. I then discussed the issue of anonymity, and let be known that it was not my intention to disclose their identity at any point, be it now or in the future, and that any names mentioned in the course of the interview (other than my own) would be changed, hence the use of pseudonyms such as Blue, Pretty, Blacker, Fat Larry and so forth. In the eventuality of the issue of criminal participation being raised, I made it clear that any names, locations or circumstantial information related to such events would be edited in transcripts. Therefore, they would have no reason to feel that any incriminating information would be passed to a third party (Jacobs, in Wright & Hobbs, 2006).

Some asked if they could smoke cigarettes/cannabis or consume alcohol during the interview. I did not object to this as it was not my place to challenge their preferred form of personal indulgence, and my primary aim was for them to behave as naturally and unaffectedly as possible; so if this was their normal mode of behaviour, and it assisted in helping the interview proceed smoothly, then I held no objection (Esterberg, 2002). Before I began recording the session, I prompted some light-hearted banter related to current events or sport, in order to allow the respondent to chat, and ease into the process. This was quite easy to do, although I did notice the vibe change slightly once the respondent became aware that he was being recorded, which was fully understandable, and in my experience, perfectly normal. I was conscious that the recording device was only able to record what I could hear, and not what I could see, therefore it was imperative that I wrote a debriefing report of the interview as soon as possible, in order to recapture the experience. In unrelated interviews conducted previously, I had taken stage notes whilst interviewing, but found that this distracted the respondent, and diminished eye contact, which is a crucial factor to keep in mind during personal engagement with West Indian men – their eyes may frequently wander away from yours, but it is important that your eyes focus on them. Within the debriefing report, I made the point of using evaluative nouns and adjectives, and noted obvious forms of non-verbal communication that were used.

Transcribing the interviews took place soon after they were conducted, so as not to lose the 'feel' and the emotional content of the process (Fielding, 2001). Transcribing interviews was of course very time-consuming and monotonous, but not without its benefits, as it allowed me to mentally revisit the exchanges, and further evaluate this privileged insight with a 'new eye'. As a result I was pleased with the fluidity of the exchanges, and was satisfied with the continued development of my craft as an ethnographer by learning how to listen (Back, 2007).

Quickly I discovered that qualitative analysis with a group of which one is a part is not as simple as I first imagined. The issue of trust, between me as the researcher and the interviewee as the conveyer of information, was of critical importance. I had to trust that the information the respondents imparted to me was a fair assessment of their reality, and correspondingly the respondents needed reassurance that the information they were communicating would not be misrepresented, distorted or adulterated (this was mentioned to me on a number of occasions). Respondents mentioned that they felt at ease talking about themselves and their lives to another West Indian, and they might not have felt *as* comfortable discussing intimacies with a researcher of another ethnicity or racial group.

However, there were occasions when I felt that interviewees assumed that because we shared the same ethnicity, their life stories would be instantly understood. For example, responses to topics such as interracial relationships and the police often felt constrained, as perhaps they felt I was in agreement with what they perceived as a standardised and collective black view on such matters. Had I been of a different gender or race, I believe topics such as these might have been explained in greater depth without the need for follow-up questions. That said, had I been of a different gender or racial group, then possibly some of the offshoot subjects I encountered might not have been raised at all.

As the interview process unfolded, I increasingly became aware how the thesis was evolving, as with every interview conducted, and every exchange that took place, I unearthed some interesting additional avenues of investigation that I had not bargained for. As with most ethnographers I have conferred with since, this can spur a temptation to stray and even digress from the original research intentions, which is common when compiling life stories and oral testaments. It then becomes a fine balancing act in which, on the one hand, one requests that the subject is open and expressive, but on the other, one has to be attentive enough to recognise when the interview is in danger of wandering off track (Noakes & Wincup, 2009). There were topics that I noticed respondents were frank in commenting on – crime was one such. This, for me, was unsurprising, for two reasons. First, black men, by virtue of belonging to a criminalised population, often have a police story to tell. Second, those with a history of criminality often have no qualms in making known their criminal exploits when questioned on a one-to-one basis. According to Goffman (1969), such individuals sometimes use ethnographic interaction as a counselling session, to relieve themselves of long-held secrets in order to disavow their wrongdoing, or to embellish and aggrandise their criminal past. Hobbs (1988) highlights the case of Keith as an example of this:

He told one group that he had earned money in the past as an enforcer. On another occasion he informed dumbstruck drinkers that he was an ex-captain of the British Junior Boxing team . . . His tough talk, ridiculous boasts, and unwanted advice were tolerated solely because of sympathy.

(Hobbs, 1988:144)

At times I felt that the interview process acted as a way for some men to give vent to the frustration and anger they felt toward society. There were occasions where invective and expletive language were used in reference to women and the education and criminal justice systems. For instance, during one interview a respondent became visibly aggravated whilst recounting a past event, and took to his feet brandishing an illegal weapon that had been concealed on his person, then in an animated fashion demonstrated his feelings towards police officers. Revisiting this emotionally charged event left him in tears, and brought the interview to an abrupt end. Interviews such as these clearly demonstrated the need for some men to unfasten feelings of frustration that had been contained for a protracted period.

Limitations

Overall, I was pleased with both the data collected and the manner in which it enhanced the intentions of my research. However, what threatened to limit the depth and intensity of the data was something I had not given thought to or bargained for, and that had to do with the issues of reflexivity and positionality. Had my investigation centred on a group unrelated to me, although access might have perhaps been restricted, I believe a socio-psychological attachment would not have existed, which would possibly produce a value-free objective analysis. However, being part of the subject group under investigation made the already difficult job of neutrality even more problematic (Klockars, in Weppner, 1977). Bourdieu (1984) expands on this by speaking of ethnographic inscription, and the significance of the outsider within, and stresses that although there exists a privileged status between the interviewer and the interviewee, by virtue of them sharing a similar worldview, the balance of power between these individuals becomes weighted in favour of the interviewer, as ultimately he/she goes on to analyse and document what is being recorded. The responsibility then is held by the interviewer to portray the subject group in a favourable manner, without tarnishing the reputation of his or her own community. This was constantly at the forefront of my mind, as the voices of these men were on occasions my voice. I felt that this bicultural analysis placed me in a position of huge personal and professional responsibility, where my conclusions would be scrutinised not only by non-West Indian or non-black audiences who wished to gain an insight into this culture, but by West Indians as well, in order to assess whether I had accurately presented the subtle nuances of Caribbean culture.

Conclusion

This chapter explains how the research for the project was carried out and how it was intended to develop the existing social commentary and academic enquiry of the post-*Windrush* generation in Britain. The methodology employed included three main imperatives. First, to document the narratives of West Indian men in Britain. Second, to recognise the experiences of these men from their own point of view and conceptualise these expressions within broader social contexts. However, the final and perhaps most important aim was to highlight the importance of positionality within ethnographic research. Therefore, it was vital that I use methods that addressed all the above aims, and keep in mind that although the data collected was inclusive of the voices of the respondents, the analysis of the data was mine.

Upon reflection, the interview process was both challenging and frustrating at times, but straightforward and rewarding at others. I learnt a lot about myself both personally and professionally in terms of cultivating patience, and learning how to listen first and speak last. I also gained a greater level of appreciation for the intricacies and complexities associated with compiling and analysing research data, which complemented the intensive training I received by virtue of an Economic and Social Research Council (ESRC) scholarship awarded via the department of Sociology at the University of Essex, and the time spent as a visiting Scholar in the department of African American studies at Yale University.

The ethnographic process taught me that answers to our questions do not always fit into nice, neat prescribed boxes, and that sometimes we do not get any answers at all. I quickly became aware of the chaotic nature of qualitative study, and proved that tenacity, organisation and a willingness to roll with the punches are the keys to completing any worthwhile form of ethnography. The methods outlined within this chapter have constructed a framework for a portrait of the post-*Windrush* generation over the past forty years, which I shall now showcase.

Notes

1 Operation Trident was a Metropolitan Police initiative commissioned to proactively investigate gun crime in black communities. It began in 1999 after a spate of firearm-related incidents in Newham, Brent and Lambeth.
2 Operation Trafalgar was a Metropolitan Police initiative tasked with investigating gun crime in London.
3 1968 Section 5 Firearm Act Amendment (6) 2004 recommends a five-year minimum sentence for illegal possession of a firearm.
4 A pseudonym for the East London location where Hobbs's fieldwork was carried out.

References

Anderson, E. (1976) *A Place on the Corner*, Chicago: University of Chicago.
Anderson, E. (1999) *Code of the Streets: Decency, Violence and the Moral Life of the Inner City*, New York: Norton.

Back, L. (2007) *The Art of Listening*, Oxford: Berg.

Becker, H. S. (1998) *Tricks of the Trade: How to Think about Research While You're Doing It*, Chicago & London: The University of Chicago Press.

Bourdieu, P. (1984) *Distinction: A Social Critique of the Judgement of Taste*, London: Routledge.

Brewer, J. D. (2000) *Ethnography*, Buckingham: Open University Press.

British Sociological Association (March 2002) *Statement of Ethical Practice*, Durham: British Sociological Association.

Bruner, J. (1987) 'Life as a Narrative', *Social Research*, 54(1): 11–32.

Esterberg, K. G. (2002) *Qualitative Methods in Social Research*, Boston: McGraw Hill.

Fielding, N. (2001) 'Ethnography', in Gilbert, N. (ed.), *Researching Social Life*, London: Sage.

Goffman, E. (1969) *The Presentation of Self in Everyday Life*, London: Allen Lane.

Gunst, L. (2004) *Born Fi Dead: A Journey through the Jamaican Posse Underworld*, New York: Henry Holt & Co.

Hall, S. (1973) *Encoding and Decoding in the Television Discourse*, Birmingham: Centre for Contemporary Cultural Studies.

Hesse-Biber, S. (2006) *The Handbook of Feminist Research Theory & Praxis*, Thousand Oaks: Sage.

Hobbs, D. (1988) *Doing the Business*, Oxford: Oxford University Press.

Hobbs, D. & May, T. (1993) *Interpreting the Field: Accounts of Ethnography*, Oxford: Oxford University Press.

Home Office (2003) *Home Office Recorded Crime Dataset*, London: HMSO.

Jacobs, B. A. (2006) 'The case for dangerous fieldwork', in Hobbs, D. & Wright, R. (eds), *The Sage Handbook of Fieldwork*, Thousand Oaks: Sage, pp. 157–168.

Lee Malcolm, J. (2004) *Guns & Violence: The English Experience*, Boston: Harvard University Press.

Mason, J. (2002) *Qualitative Researching*, London: Sage.

McLagan, G. (2006) *Guns and Gangs: The Inside Story of the War on Our Streets*, London: Allison & Busby.

McNeil, P. & Chapman, J. (2005) *Research Methods*, Abingdon: Routledge.

McRobbie, A. & Thornton, S. (2009) 'Rethinking moral panic in multi-mediated social worlds', in Muncie, J., Hughes, G. & McLaughlin, E. (eds), *Youth Justice: Critical Readings*, London: Sage, pp. 559–574.

Noakes, L. & Wincup, E. (2009) *Criminological Research: Understanding Qualitative Methods*, London: Sage.

Operation Trident Reactive Operations (2002) London: Metropolitan Police/Home Office.

Pryce, K. (1979) *Endless Pressure*, Bristol: Bristol Classical Press.

Punch, M. (1996) *Dirty Business: Exploring Corporate Misconduct*, London: Sage.

Silverman, D. (2000) *Doing Qualitative Research: A Practical Handbook*, London: Sage.

Soloway, I. & Walters, J. (1977) 'Workin' the Corner: The Ethics and Legality of Ethnographic Fieldwork Among Active Heroin Addicts', in Weppner, R. S. (ed.), *Street Ethnography: Selected Studies of Crime and Drug Use in Natural Settings*, Beverly Hills & London: Sage, pp. 159–178.

Stein, M. (2006) 'Your Place or Mine: The Geography of Social Research', in Hobbs, D. & Wright, R. (eds), *The Sage Handbook of Fieldwork*, Thousand Oaks: Sage, pp. 59–75.

Van Maanen, J. (1988) *Tales from the Field*, Chicago: The University of Chicago Press.

Walsh, P. (2003) *Gang War; The Inside Story of the Manchester Gangs*, Reading: Milo Books.

Weppner, R. S. (1977) *Street Ethnography: Selected Studies of Crime and Drug Use in Natural Settings*, Beverly Hills & London: Sage.

Whyte, W. (1984) *Learning from the Field: A Guide from Experience*, Beverly Hills & London: Sage.

Wright, R. & Decker, S. (1994) *Burglars on the Job: Streetlife and Residential Break-ins*, Boston: North Eastern University Press.

Wright, R. & Hobbs, D. (2006) *The Sage Handbook of Fieldwork*, Thousand Oaks: Sage.

Chapter 4

Black British self-concept

Blackness and Britishness are complex concepts to unpack. In fact, identity politics are notoriously difficult to assess as they are fluid in nature and are constantly in flux, and, as we will see, within them lie ideas that challenge a number of established sociological perspectives. However, what has remained an invariable feature within the evolving concepts of both blackness and Britishness is a pathological response to racial and social indifference. A recent example was the United Kingdom European Membership Referendum of June 2016, and the subsequent vote to leave the European Union (more commonly known as Brexit), which propelled nationalist ideas of belonging to become fixed within public and political debate. This chapter will attempt to unravel, and where possible simplify, these issues in reference to black cultural identity in Britain.

The better-known academic literature surrounding blackness in Europe and Britain is widely reliant on a canon of commentary delivered by exponents such as Fanon (1967, 1963), Sivanandan (1974), Gilroy (1987, 1993a, 1993b) and Hall (1973, 1978, 1980, 1997). In comparison, African-American literature related to blackness covers a wide spectrum of socio-economic and political perspectives. This is rarely inclusive of the Diasporised, but focuses primarily on blacks within the borders of North America. Similarly Caribbean scholars of renown such as Eric Williams, Walter Rodney and Louise Bennett-Coverley admirably raise issues related to Caribbean cultural identity but frequently omit an in-depth analysis of Caribbean peoples in Europe, which is often left to be undertaken by poets and novelists such as Kamau Brathwaite, V. S. Naipaul, George Lamming and Sam Selvon.

> We wear the mask that grins and lies,
> It hides our cheeks and shades our eyes, –
> This debt we pay to human guile;
> With torn and bleeding hearts we smile,
> And mouth with myriad subtleties.
> Why should the world be over-wise,
> In counting all our tears and sighs?

Nay, let them only see us, while
We wear the mask.
                    (Dunbar, 1892:167)

Here Paul Lawrence Dunbar, like Fanon later on, reminds us of the mask that frequently accompanies the problematic and constricted nature of racial identity.

Within the field I have identified various factors related to the crisis of identity that many of West Indian descent in Britain face. There are clearly issues of doubleness, intermixture and duality evident within the lives of these men. Be it British, Caribbean or African, each identity strives at intermittent junctures for dominance, which according to subjects themselves, often proves to be problematic:

> I'm a West Indian, not African or British – never! Being British is something you have to feel in your heart and gives a feeling that you belong. I don't feel like I belong. I find it hard to understand why some black people think that they are British, when there are loads of white people who don't think that black people can be British. Over here [in Britain] it's the mixture of the black mind and the white mind, and that messes us up.
>
> (Red)

In reference to European cultural identity and African identity, Ture and Hamilton (1992) suggest that one cannot help but notice the manner in which these cultures are diametrically opposed. Gilroy (1993a) suggests that where these identities clash, a hybrid concept of self emerges, often characterised by multi-faceted forms of consciousness that develop and relentlessly vie for a position of dominance. For Gilroy, cultural identities are not simply made up of concepts such as language, dress or linguistic inflection; they are tied to broader notions of nation, nationality, national belonging and nationalism, all of which are concepts that are difficult for those who are othered to internalise, as they are ideals dictated by the state. As a result, we noticed during the 1980s that the majority of the post-*Windrush* generation purposely shunned notions of Britishness, in contrast to the very few who eagerly strove to integrate and be accepted by the host culture. Carrington illustrates this point further, quoting the former world heavyweight boxing champion Frank Bruno:

> I was a dedicated fan of Maggie Thatcher's when she was in No. 10 Downing Street. I have never met anybody as strong-minded and as confident as she was. Just by her very presence she could make you feel a foot taller at the thought of being British.
>
> (Carrington, in Owusu, 2000:147)

As newly arrived settlers do, the *Windrush* migrants chose to develop their own sense of cultural identity in Britain by utilising those aspects of West

Indian culture which they deemed to be most useful within a British context. Factors such as respectability, discipline, family configuration and religion, which were core to Caribbean values, had an established place within their adopted British lifestyles (Pryce, 1979; Monrose, 2017). Other significant aspects were also evident, particularly among those who were politically aware. For example, Gilroy (1987) mentions that blacks in Britain, particularly in the 1960s and 1970s, were intrinsically anti-capitalist, and carried with them from the Caribbean the ideals of communal participation.

One of the more useful tools for examining the transformation of cultural identity in Britain is music. Whereas in the 1970s and early 1980s music of choice for black youths relied heavily on the attachment to the Caribbean within the genre of reggae, towards the end of the 1980s we witnessed a shift: black Britons were finding their own voices by developing homegrown forms of musical expression. Whilst *Windrush* arrivals introduced and contributed to new ways of procuring musical spaces, via sound systems,[1] blues dances and shubeens,[2] the post-*Windrush* generation developed new forms of music to be played within the aforementioned settings. Lovers Rock[3] for example, was arguably the first artistic triumph to highlight the creative vibrancy of the post-*Windrush* generation, whilst concurrently promoting a positive aesthetic of blackness within the British imagination. Henry (2006) elaborates on the significance of this:

> Black music creates that space in which alternative notions of being black, both positive and negative, can be discursively debated and disseminated across the urban landscape. Therefore London can be regarded as a nodal point in a multicultural system of creative processes.
>
> (Henry, 2006:93)

East London to East New York

As mentioned earlier, issues of identity related to African-Americans are liberally utilised to examine issues related to black British identity. We know, however, that this is of limited use, and, as I will go on to show, does not confront the vast differences that are evident between these groups. To exemplify this I will briefly present a narrative of an African-American's experience in Britain, and then go on to present my own experiences in undertaking research as a black Briton in America.

Harvard Professor Henry Louis Gates Jr. provides useful insight into the experience of an African-American scholar visiting Britain. Amongst the hustle and bustle of London streets, Gates seeks directions to an appointment. Upon approaching the first black face seen, he's startled to find that although they both speak English, communication is difficult. Gates goes on to further describe his experience of being a black man in London. He recounts a visit to a shubeen, and notes that the atmosphere therein was not one of celebration, jubilation and jollification as expected, but one of uptightness and harsh expressions:

> On Saturday, the younger generation of Britain's recent immigrants would gather at some vacant house that had recently been 'liberated' for the occasion, the electricity and gas reconnected for an evening of bacchana-lia. It was called 'going blues', and although the site changed from week to week, you rarely had to ask where it was being held; you could hear it half a block away, as the reggae thudded through the adjoining council housing. You paid your twenty pence at the door and entered into swelter-ing Caribbean heat. The floors trembled from the enormous bass loud-speakers. Upstairs people queued for food and Johnny Walker served in Coke cans. Everybody was smoking Ganja: You could get high just from breathing. But what always struck me was how joyless it all seemed: nobody spoke or even laughed. Expressions were hard, affectless.
>
> (Gates, 1997, in Owusu, 2000:170)

Gates concludes that blacks in Britain are discontented, victims of unrelenting social pressure. He views occasions such as these, which are meant for jollifi-cation, as essentially joyless, and a reflection of life for blacks in Britain. The phenomenon of the blues dance for Gates was just that, a mirror image of the 'blues' (downheartedness), interlaced within the daily lives of disaffected blacks in Britain. However, from a black British perspective his view of these occasions can be challenged:

> All roads led to the blues dance. It was our thing. It was safe. It was an extension of our front room, and the vibes was always nice.
>
> (Monrose, 2016:78)

This brief inclusion of Gates's narrative is important, as it critically challenges notions of equivalence, homogeneity and sameness, which are often levelled at blacks throughout the black Atlantic, and clearly demonstrates the difficulties associated with issues related to black identities. It is crucial to note the vast differences between blacks in Europe and blacks in America, as we must keep in mind that not only are blacks markedly more numerous in America than in Britain, but the legacy of mass black presence is also significantly longer. The African-American has to a great extent become ingrained in many aspects of American life. A good example is the existence of an established and widely visible African-American middle-class stratum, whereas a corresponding defined and located black British middle-class assemblage has yet to be fully recognised (Rollock et al., 2013). Additionally, political events such as the Civil Rights movement helped shape the formation of an African-American political and cultural identity, whereas there has been no corresponding Civil

Rights movement or mobilisation in Britain. This all makes for an interesting comparative insight into two groups who share many similarities but also many differences.

A segment of my PhD fieldwork was spent as a visiting scholar in America, enrolled at the Department of African American Studies at Yale University, specifically to examine and consider issues of racial identity. Although I had visited America many times previously, this was the first occasion I proactively sought to utilise my sociological eye in such an exacting manner. Like Gates in London, I was surprised at what I discovered. First I found that the vast majority of African-Americans I met defined themselves as middle-class, and in my view held no real affinity with the working class. Moreover, echoing Frank Bruno's patriotic stance (quoted earlier by Carrington), this assemblage openly and eagerly stated that they were proud to be identified as Americans. In fact, many lauded their American status as both a privilege and a virtue. However, I attributed this to my Ivy League location, and the fact that I was amongst those Du Bois termed the 'talented tenth' – the black American leadership class.

In order to test this theory more comprehensively, I decided to venture else-where and pose similar questions. I headed towards the Eastern Seaboard to established African-American spaces such as Harlem in New York City, and East New York, in areas such as Brownsville in Brooklyn. To my astonishment I was met by an analogous response to that in New Haven, Connecticut (the location of Yale). I was surprised, since in my experience blacks in Britain, as we will see, ground their racial identity in relation to the place of their parents' birth. Blue, Blacker, Fat Larry and Gilly, along with others, identified them-selves as Jamaican, St Lucian or Dominican, even though they were born in Britain, whereas many African-Americans, who, like their British counterparts, might have parents and grandparents from the 'Islands'(the Caribbean), failed to openly acknowledge this as part of their lineage. Some whom I met on the streets of Harlem, such as Jughead, even went as far as referring to those from the Caribbean as 'monkeys':[4]

> I'm an American through and through, brother, and proud to be one too. I don't have no links to those monkeys over there on them islands.
>
> (Jughead)

This brief examination demonstrates that African-American and black British identities differ, and it is clumsy to embrace received knowledge that suggests blackness is standardised and uniform. Differences in historical residence, social mobility and self- or group identity easily displace suggestions of racial and ethnic homogeneity. This also shows that in America, unlike in Britain, social position easily eclipses race.

The emergence of black-centred intellectualism in Britain during the 1970s helped to address the concerns associated with black cultural identities. The Centre for Contemporary Cultural Studies at Birmingham University, commonly referred to as the Birmingham School,[5] remains the most prominent and best known for the development of cultural studies and for the belated emergence of race-oriented intellectualism in Britain. Prior to its impetus and contribution to knowledge, issues pertaining to ethnicity had yet to be debated comprehensively, and the matter of race functioned simply in binary terms of black and white. Non-white populations such as South Asians, and at times the Irish, were considered black both politically and administratively.

It is here we see the early work of Stuart Hall pressing for a directed and accurate definition of so-called minority ethnic groups (Hall, 1973). According to Hall, the idea of race was an ever-present reality, all around us at all times, and ethnicity by default was crucial within any debate on race. Moreover, for Hall, the *Windrush* arrivals' quest for Britishness was an unobtainable goal that was even harder for their offspring to achieve, who, unlike themselves, had no real sense of escape from the far-reaching tentacles of everyday racial discrimination. Blacks born in Britain were acutely aware that their presence was undesirable, and therefore adopted a consciousness that suggested that their real 'home' was in the West Indies, despite having no first-hand experience of life there. These individuals were not divorced from society *per se*, as they often felt, but were living within a larger postcolonial narrative, acknowledged or not, and, due to the social exclusion they faced, were forced to retreat into their own sense of *blackness*, and take on the political identity of the Caribbean. The intricacies associated with racial identities are superbly illustrated by Hall, when we notice that much of his work and commentary is reflexive and tied to his own personal experiences.

Additionally, Hall points out that racial identity discourse is not simply made up of binary variables that are presented as black and white, but is positioned within larger and more complex narratives, highlighting that West Indian people are not exclusively black – some are white, and many more are Asian, meaning that the complexities imbedded within issues of cultural and racial identity are often informed by colonial and postcolonial imperatives. This means that some ideas surrounding *blackness* are also measured by the quotient of melanin and phenotypical composition – octoroon, quadroon, mulatto or shadism, if you will, which in turn impinge on concepts of social status and class. Red elaborates:

> In the Caribbean, go into the hotels and look, all the staff are black and the managers are clear skinned, the banks are the same. It's a crazy thing to say, but it still happens. You get the darkest skinned person, who is the smartest of all applicants, and he still wouldn't get the job, they would prefer to give it to the less bright but clear skin one.
>
> (Red)

Sivanandan (1974), like Hall, makes a lasting contribution to the debate on cultural identities in Britain by stressing that the West Indian in Britain is a creature of two worlds, and as a result belongs to none. He observes that the black man in Britain is caught between the world of the 'Mother Country' (Britain) and the world of his ancestry (Africa/Caribbean); he either accepts his culture or rejects it as a means of survival:

> For a while he succeeds in holding these two worlds together, the outer and the inner, deriving the best of both. But the forces of nationalism on the one hand, and the virus of colonial privilege on the other, drive him once more to the margin of existence.
>
> (Sivanandan, 1974, in Owusu, 2000:70)

Sivanandan goes on to suggest that the language of the colonised also belongs elsewhere, as does the colonial education he receives, which is essentially culturally deterministic, and relegates his own culture and historical narrative in favour of high culture, which habitually depicts the black male as a tragic figure. The writing of William Shakespeare provides an example in works such as *Othello*, and the characterisation of Caliban in *The Tempest* (2007 edition). For Sivanandan, the position of the displaced black male is untenable if he requires that his status be equated to that of the British:

> Outwardly he favours that part of him which is turned towards his native land. He puts on the garb of nationalism, vows a return to tradition. He helps design a national flag, composes a people's anthem. He puts up with the beat of the Tom- Tom, and the ritual of the circumcision ceremony. But privately he lives in the manner of his masters, affecting their style and their values, assuming their privileges and status.
>
> (Sivanandan, 1974, in Owusu, 2000:70)

For D'Aguiar (2000) the crisis of cultural identity for blacks in Britain can be attributed to a shift from a majority group, as they were in the Caribbean, into occupying a minority status, as they did in Britain. This crisis is maintained by the twin loyalties and the dual demands that are placed upon the newly arrived, who, as pointed out earlier, wrestle with the notion of inbetweenness, and lone status. D'Aguiar outlines his own experience of arriving in Britain from Guyana:

> London was spoiled for me by my belief that one day I would not return to Guyana, and when that was no longer true, by a feeling that London did not belong to me, could never belong to me on account of my race, my minority status. A white majority made me aware on a daily basis that I was a visitor, a guest whose invitation to the club could at any moment's notice be withdrawn and the friendly standoffish bouncers would suddenly turn menacing.
>
> (D'Aguiar in Owusu, 2000:197)

These sentiments encapsulate the fundamental nature of doubleness felt by members of the post-*Windrush* generation. Fire states, 'The only time I feel English is when I'm in the West Indies, and the only time I feel West Indian is when I'm in England'. This becomes increasingly complex when we notice that the individuals who were born in the Caribbean and then came to Britain in their formative years, after being schooled within an educational system rooted in colonialist ideologies, had a greater theoretical understanding of 'Britishness' than their British-born contemporaries. For some theirs is an identity rooted in their place of birth, with a desire to return 'back home' at some point, and having no intention of being superannuated in a country of which they feel no part:

> If my son was older I would have gone back already. My eyes have been open to many things, and I've seen too many of my uncles die here [in England]. I don't want to be old and alone in the cold, I'd rather be in the warm and be healthy and accepted.
>
> (Mr Brown)

It is only recently that we notice middle-aged black populations born in Britain refer to themselves as British. Their theoretical status as British has been acknowledged to a certain extent, but they have rejected practical notions of Britishness, mainly because of the mechanisms that excluded them from participation in the established ideals of being British whilst growing up. Art, music and sport, more than political policy, have helped to forge an angle of acceptance. King (2000) suggests that sport (football) allows blacks to shed the shackles of their blackness, in order for a cloak of 'whiteness' to be worn, particularly if they are willing to adopt the role of the 'Whiteman':

> On one level playing the Whiteman means doing what the white working class players have had to traditionally do in football. Yet this should not detract from the fact a process of racialisation is taking place: in order to belong you have to behave like white players, or at least act on their terms.
>
> (King, 2000:2)

King's statement is both insightful and useful, but adopting the role of 'Whiteman' comes with an array of attachments and constraints, particularly in terms of media representation. For example, the black sportsman who is successful and on top of his game is lauded as British. However, with any misdemeanour in his private life or his performance on the field his 'Britishness' is instantly rescinded, and his non-British status is handed back post-haste. The treatment by the news media of England and Manchester City footballer Raheem Sterling is a good example.

Conclusion

> Sometimes when I go back and I see some of the people that never left, I wonder if I was better off than them. They spent their whole life on a Caribbean island, and never had to deal with the problems of race and racism.
>
> (Red)

Identity is fluid, and is over time subject to transformation, often in response to broader social contexts and political imperatives. Cultural, ethnic and racial identity formation acted as an integral component in the lives of the post-*Windrush* generation, because, as shown in this chapter, at some point in their lives, ambiguities and contradictions exposed their indeterminate state of consciousness. Over time, however, they carefully crafted their own cultural identities. Significant glimpses of this reclamation and self-definition are seen in, for example, the appearance of Rastafari in the 1970s and 1980s. This is important as one of the first steps on the ladder of regaining the level of self-determination that was lacking among the *Windrush* arrivals, who for the most part were content to realise their five-year plan in Britain. The post-*Windrush* generation didn't have a five-year economic plan to realise; they were here to stay, and were not only forced to challenge issues pertaining to cultural identity but, as we will see in the following chapter, also compelled to address established gendered representations associated with black maleness and manhood.

Notes

1 Mobile high-powered discotheque. Vincent George Forbes, aka 'Duke Vin the Champion', was the first sound system owner of note in Britain and Europe, established in 1954. Vin was one of the first deejays on the legendary sound system 'Tom the Great Sebastian' in Jamaica.
2 Unlicensed premises that charge an entrance fee and sell alcohol and food. Also known as a 'push in' or blues party/blues dance, or simply a 'blues'.
3 British-produced romantically themed reggae developed in the late 1970s to early 1980s.
4 A derogatory term for African Caribbean people used by African-Americans.
5 Celebrated centre of black intellectualism in Britain, particularly in the 1970s and 1980s, and responsible for the development of Cultural studies that rely heavily on the work of Matthew Arnold (1869), which recognises the importance of culture within philosophical, political and sociological study. Arnold's work is enhanced by synthesising Althusser's (1969, 1976) theoretical stance on subjectivity, in order to explain the position of subcultural groups in society. Similarly, hegemony, according to Gramsci (1971), can be transposed and framed within a context of identity, class, race and culture (see Willis, 1977; McRobbie, 1995).

References

Althusser, L. (1969) *For Marx*, Harmondsworth: Penguin.

Althusser, L. (1976) 'Reply to John Lewis', in *Essays in Self Criticism*, London: New Left Books, pp. 33–99.

Arnold, M. (1869) *Culture and Anarchy: An Essay in Political and Social Criticism*, London: Cornhill Magazine.

Carrington, B. (2000) 'Double Consciousness and the Black British Athlete', in Owusu, K. (ed.), *Black British Culture & Society: A Text Reader*, London: Routledge, pp. 133–156.

D'Aguiar, F. (2000) 'Home is Always Elsewhere: Individual and Communal Regulative Capacities of Loss', in Owusu, K. (ed.), *Black British Culture & Society: A Text Reader*, London: Routledge, pp. 195–206.

Dunbar, P. (1892) *Lyrics of a Lowly Life*, New York: Citadel Press.

Fanon, F. (1963) *The Wretched of the Earth*, New York: Grove Press.

Fanon, F. (1967) *Black Skin, White Masks*, New York: Grove Press.

Gates, H. L., Jnr. (1997) *The Classic Slave Narratives: The Life of Olaudah Equiano. The History of Mary Prince. Narrative of the Life of Frederick Douglass. Incidents in the Life of a Slave Girl*, New York: Signet Classic.

Gilroy, P. (1987) *There Ain't No Black in the Union Jack: The Cultural Politics of Race and Nation*, London: Hutchinson Education.

Gilroy, P. (1993a) *The Black Atlantic: Modernity and Double Consciousness*, London: Verso.

Gilroy, P. (1993b) *Small Acts: Thoughts on the Politics of Black Cultures*, London: Serpent's Tail.

Gramsci, A. (1971) *Selection from Prison Notebooks*, London: Lawrence & Wishart.

Hall, S. (1973) *Encoding and Decoding in the Television Discourse*, Birmingham: Centre for Contemporary Cultural Studies.

Hall, S. (1978) *Policing the Crisis: Mugging, the State and Law and Order*, London: Hutchinson.

Hall, S. (1980) *Drifting into Law and Order Society*, London: Cobden Trust.

Hall, S. (1997) 'Frontlines and Backyards: The Terms of Change', in Owusu, K. (ed.), *Black British Culture & Society: A Text Reader*, London: Routledge, pp. 127–129.

Henry, W. (2006) *What the Deejay Said*, London: Nu Beyond.

King, C. (2000) *Play the White Man: The Theatre of Racialised Performance in the Institutions of Soccer*, London: Goldsmiths College, University of London.

McRobbie, A. (1995) *Post Modernism and Popular Culture*, London: Routledge.

Monrose, K. (2016) 'Struggling, Juggling and Street Corner Hustling: The Street Economy of Newham's Black Community', in Antonopoulos, G. (ed.), *Illegal Entrepreneurship, Organized Crime and Social Control, Essays in Honor of Professor Dick Hobbs*, Geneva: Springer, pp. 73–84.

Monrose, K. (2017) 'Shame, Scandal and Respectability Amongst the Children of *Windrush* Generation: A Scholarly Omission', in Hobbs, D. (ed.), *Mischief, Morality and Mobs: Essays in Honour of Geoffrey Pearson*, New York & Abingdon: Routledge, pp. 59–82.

Owusu, K. (2000) *Black British Culture & Society: A Text Reader*, London: Routledge.

Pryce, K. (1979) *Endless Pressure*, Bristol: Bristol Classical Press.

Rollock, N., Gillborn, D., Vincent, C. & Ball, J. (2013) *The Colour of Class: The Educational Strategies of the Black Middle Classes*, New York & Abingdon: Routledge.
Shakespeare, W. (2007) *The Tempest*, London: Penguin Classics.
Sivanandan, A. (1974) 'The Liberation of the Black Intellectual', in Owusu, K. (ed.), *Black British Culture & Society: A Text Reader*, London: Routledge, pp. 70–80.
Ture, K. & Hamilton, C. (1992) *Black Power: The Politics of Liberation in America*, New York: Pelican Books.
Willis, P. (1977) *Learning to Labour*, London: Saxon House.

Chapter 5

Being a black man

British commentary on black masculinities continues to be affixed to issues such as crime and deviance. However, what is commonly omitted from structural inequality explanations of 'black criminality' is the unmentionable legacy of post-colonialism and empire. In contrast, sociological research surrounding black masculinity delivered from North America is often characterised by daily interactions of black men within their adopted spaces. Therefore topics such as social position and social class can effortlessly tie gendered issues to wider sociological imperatives.

Such a synthesis is often not presented within British narratives, simply because black British political and social mobility is still relatively new in comparison to that of African-Americans.[1] Moreover the over-policing of blacks since Commonwealth migration to Britain in the 1940s and the resulting episodes of resistance mean that a number of political issues related to black men are often discussed only in reference to their relationship with the criminal justice system. Although academic research and literary commentary conducted on blacks in Britain has a lengthy legacy, the main bodies of work that address everyday sociological issues of black life are limited. Consequently there is a chasm in the authoritative and effective investigation of black masculinities in Britain. This is of concern particularly as many of the texts that observe the everyday lives of black males habitually focus on black youth, and ignore black adult or middle-aged populations in Britain (Alexander, 2001; Gunter, 2010; White, 2017).

The black masculine

The use of an umbrella term such as 'masculinity' is misleading, as it is suggests a 'one size fits all' definition of maleness that is grounded in a stencil of western hegemony, which is often identified by features such as assertiveness, dominance, competitiveness and violence. I suggest that 'masculinities' is a far more suitable designation, as masculinities are not homogeneous and uniform, but are adopted according to class position, race and sexuality, and can be categorised in three groups – complicit, subordinate and marginalised.

Complicit masculinity is commonly typified by the characterisation of the 'new man' – a male who openly displays his 'feminine side' and is said to be liberated from the confines of patriarchy. Subordinate masculinity is frequently used to define homosexual men, and stresses that although homosexuality today enjoys a greater level of tolerance than ever, it is still at times highly stigmatised. But it is the last category, marginalised masculinity that will be the essential concern of this chapter. Marginalised masculinity, according to Connell (1987, 1995), is shaped by economics, social class and race, factors that, I will go on to argue, have had a profound effect on shaping the life course of black men in Britain.

Accessible popular historical narratives by authors such as James (2001), Equiano (1998) and Douglass (1845), whilst providing the reader with an insight into the seemingly never-ending struggle for black emancipation and liberty, have also given the enquirer a broader understanding of black masculinities. Slave narratives provide, though not overtly, a reference point by which black masculinities can be observed over the passage of time. Du Bois (1903, 1907) and Frazier (1940, 1963) also provide reliable coverage of black life during antebellum and Reconstruction eras, particularly in reference to men. Both Du Bois and Frazier indicate how black men successfully provided for their families, and formulated a thriving economic structure, by developing a notion of self-reliance, in response to widespread social disadvantage.

Feminist perspectives have also significantly contributed to the study of black masculinities and maleness, and have provided insightful and noteworthy commentaries that offer a greater understanding of this branch of learning. Female interpretations of masculinities are extremely relevant, as it is women who are often subject to the wider apparatus of patriarchy. For instance, in the popular and ongoing debate on misogyny within reggae music, Cooper (2000) presents a considered counter-narrative on this much maligned subject. She argues that whilst these musical forms can indeed be seen as misogynist, they can be also perceived as being empowering for working-class women. She suggests that within the dancehall arena, one encounters themes that allow poor, lower-class women to visibly celebrate their sexuality and sensuality, albeit somewhat crudely at times:

> The recurring references in the DJ's lyrics to fleshy female body parts and oscillatory functions is not a devaluation of female sexuality; it is reclamation of active adult female sexuality from the entrapping passivity of sexless Victorian virtue.
>
> (Cooper, in Owusu, 2000:351)

This idea of reclamation, recalibration and empowerment is equally relevant to men. Majors (1993) notices the need for black men to adopt a succession of coping strategies in order to reclaim aspects of the manliness to which western hegemonic masculinity denies them access. The posturing and swaggering embodiment which Majors describes as 'cool pose' is an attempt to salvage and compensate for this lack:

> Playing cool protects one's chances of survival and enhances self-esteem. Cool pose can be used as a form of protection against white authorities. The man – police and other symbols of white authority – can be thrown off balance by carefully staged cool performance. Cool pose serves as a guide for behaviour under the kind of pressure that might occur during an encounter with the police or a boss.
>
> (Majors, 1993:93)

Majors also suggests that black men will at times, portray a measure of aloofness and detachment, in an attempt to look 'cool' and tough. For Majors, the 'cool pose' is one of the key traits of black masculinity that other commentators such as Katz (2006) go on to define as hyper- or uber-masculinity. I too have noted this in my work with both black (and working-class white) males, who co-opt similar forms of embodiment such as exaggerated gait, off-centered gaze, with external physical adornment such as piercings, tattoos and jewellery.

Despite the construction of some black masculinities to reclaim the perceived loss of manliness and to engender respect, these types of portrayals are often viewed negatively, and further alienate the black male from the mainstream. Unfortunately a number of black males assume these characteristics without being fully aware of the push-back that these limited and detached depictions can induce. In addition, they at times may allow the aggression and anger that underscore these portrayals to inveigle them into nihilistic and stereotypical forms of behaviour that reinforce representations of black men. Individuals such as Burglar are fully aware of this, but still relish the opportunity to be perceived as erratic and volatile:

> I know as soon as you see me, and the size of me, you're going to be wary, thinking 'big black man!' So I play on it and use it to my advantage. A black man don't have a lot advantages in this world so if the niceness don't work then the stereotype comes out, and then I don't give a fuck who it is in front of me. I've always been like that.
>
> (Burglar)

Burglar embraces this negative attributed identity as a response to his experience. Alexander sees these negative black masculinities, or what she terms 'the black macho', as a misapprehension and simply a pictogram for powerlessness:

> Machismo becomes a symbol of, and substitute for the lack of power rather than constituting an aspect of that power. It has thus been seen as

inauthentic and illusionary; something apart from, and opposed to the wider structures of society.

(Alexander, 1996, in Owusu, 2000:69)

Violence and the raw edge

Katz (2006) offers an interesting insight into male violence in westernised culture, and stresses that as masculinities have become progressively amplified, violence has increased (he records that 90 per cent of all violent crimes in the US are committed by men). He stresses that Western societies expect boys to be tough, physical and in control. Those who are unable to kowtow to this convention are often referred to in disparaging feminised terms such as 'pussy', 'wimp' or 'bitch'. Katz makes some additional observations that are worthy of note. For example, he highlights the manner in which playthings for male children have become increasingly manly – oversized and exaggeratedly muscular groups of action figures, for example. He points out that over the past few decades, the physiques of on-screen 'superheroes' have tripled or quadrupled in mass, to appear 'manlier'.[2] Similarly the dimensions of weapons in the possession of the male action hero have increased in contrast to those of a previous era. Comparisons are made between the original James Bond character armed with a Berretta 418 (now described as a lady's firearm) and the M60 military assault rifle, the M2 Browning machine gun and RPG (rocket propelled grenade) of Sylvester Stallone's *John Rambo*. Or the manner in which the questionable acting skills of Arnold Schwarzenegger are eclipsed by the openly promiscuous and violent nature of his caricatures.[3] For Katz, the media is crucial in the development of violent forms of masculinity into a cultural norm. However, the most significant point raised by Katz concerns the relationship between economics and masculinity. He suggests the disorderly economic structure of society has meant a life of inescapable marginalisation for some men. Individuals devoid of economic or material clout have only their physical attributes, and non-verbal prowess, as an apparatus of power. This, although convoluted in Katz's view, is an easily adopted coping strategy deployed by those outside the parameters of hegemonic masculinity, and framed within a context of violence.

So far we have seen traditional masculinities embrace concepts centred on power, control and authority; however these are factors that in the main have been denied to black men. Bowling and Phillips (2002) suggest that the social marginalisation that black men overwhelmingly encounter can also prompt a search for an alternative route by which to express and define themselves. Therefore we find black men innovating and creating substitute masculinities. Gilly, for example, despite his esteemed employment status and academic attainment, believes that black men, in order to avoid increased disparagement and disdain from wider society, are still required to adopt stereotypical masculine forms:

> Well yeah, I'm an educated bod, but I've got to be that rough diamond as well. You still need to have that raw edge. If you don't have that edge then you're looked upon as a pussyhole! My friend Dwayne, a Jamaican guy, is calm, quiet and placid, but people call him a wanker cos he don't have that raw ghetto edge, that manliness.
>
> (Gilly)

The 'raw edge' mentioned here means that some black men choose to forge a 'roadman' or 'bad boy' persona in order to negotiate a pathway commonly littered with negative stereotypes and characterisations. As a result we see forms of hyper-masculinity paraded, typified by sexual braggadocio, self-aggrandisement, untamed violence and rebellion. Collingson (1996) mentions that black men who have been structurally excluded develop and maintain hyper-masculine traits by wilfully living 'on the edge', in an almost nihilistic and self-destructive manner. The pursuit of developing a reputation for being 'bad' and acting 'mad' increases street-level status. Blue confirms these sentiments by suggesting that actions resulting in infamy, notoriety and erratic behaviour are indeed desirable. In fact, the one predictable character trait that Blue is happy to demonstrate in public is his unpredictability:

> I'm a bad man you know. Listen you're not supposed to fuck about with me because I'm an unpredictable breh [brother]. People don't really know what to expect from me.
>
> (Blue)

Anderson (1999, 2006) and Monrose (2016) maintain that the code and ethics dictated by street corner men demand particular displays of masculinity. Being able to fight, or having a reputation of being able to manage oneself physically, for example, is a primary tool to achieve heightened social kudos. Even if one is not proficient in unarmed/armed combat, the sub-cultural structure of urban street life demands masculine posturing at the very least. For such men, reputation and image within public space are of supreme importance. Because society dictates that material success and masculine prowess walk in tandem, the disenfranchised black male becomes increasingly aware that he is expected to be overtly masculine in order to be credited with worthy status. This is often counterproductive; however, as the same mechanisms that he believes transform him into a turbo-masculine entity, and impel respect will also reinforce the established negative stereotypes of black men. Black male sexualisation is one such potent example, which I will expand on in the following section.

Representation and sexualisation of the black male

Western society has, over the last fifty years, become increasingly obsessed with body composition, body type and body image (Greer, 1976). Embodiment is increasingly utilised by the advertising and marketing industries as a means of showcasing their commodities. From cigars to cars and chocolate bars, the body has been used to mesmerise, amuse and manipulate the minds of the masses. Undeniably the most potent method of commercial marketing is attached to sex (Wykes & Gunter, 2004). Regardless of the goods, implied sexual titillation is often used as the means by which that all-important deal is brokered. Women have for a long time been subjected to objectification, and their sexual exploitation has been centrally positioned within the apparatus of merchandising. The sexualisation of women has been a very successful man-oeuvre in economic terms for advertisers, who embrace beguiling maxims such as 'sex sells'. Feminists of diverse political persuasions have suggested that this wholesale sexualisation amounts to misogynistic manipulation, as it denies women all sense of humanity, and reduces them to be viewed simply as vessels of exploitative and lustful desire (Solanas, 1968; Orbach, 2006). However, the sexual objectification of the body is not only gendered; there is an overtly pre-sented racial dynamic to this discussion that I feel has not experienced as much scholarly interrogation as it deserves.

As we are aware, racial groups that fall outside the mainstream (read as white and middle-class) are often stereotypically sexualised within cultural rep-resentations orchestrated and then disseminated by the mass media. Pictograms of the sexually submissive East Asian female, the uninhibited white female, the promiscuous black female and the oversexed black male are examples of this offensive and essentialist imagery. These cultural representations have strong social ramifications, and both regulate and dictate social practices that have lasting practical effects on the groups in question. In terms of black men these representations habitually impart an image of either a highly sexualised individual or a potentially criminally inclined persona.

> The portrait of black masculinity that emerges in this work perpetually constructs men as 'failures', who are psychologically fucked up, danger-ous, violent sex maniacs whose insanity is informed by their inability to fulfil the phallocentric masculine destiny in a racist context.
>
> (hooks, 1993:89)

Welsing (1991) suggests that some black men inevitably go on to internalise these representations, and act in tandem with these communicated stereotypes. Burglar is one such example who openly views himself as a 'gyalist' or 'cocksman' (a man with many women available for his sexual gratification and use). In order to gain street-level respect, it was imperative that he played these roles:

I was a cocksman, a bedroom bully. I used to run nuff gal on road – that's how it was for me. It's like the more girls I had the most things I had, and the more things I had, was the more respect I got. Some man can't manage it but that was my thing.

(Burglar)

Historically, the black male body was commoditised as a tool of production for capitalism and oppressive regimes of colonialism. Recent history, however, has unearthed a transformation in the way black embodiment is exploited. Now it is used as a crude representation for promiscuity, virility and sexual excess. Fanon (1963, 1967) suggests that these representations strip the black male of all intellectual, rational or cerebral capacity, and instead focus on him in physical or biological terms alone (which in many ways is a remix of theories offered by key thinkers during the Enlightenment period, as outlined in Chapter 2).

Within these mythologised notions of black male sexuality lies an innate fascination with the black penis. This phallic fixation, or penis envy, is commonly vocalised in white male commentary, which, Welsing (1991) suggests, makes the white male himself feel inferior to the alleged proportions of black male genitalia. This results in the black male being eroticised and idolised, but then simultaneously despised and condemned. The prodigiously well-endowed black male, when explicitly expressed in pornographic literature and film, is often referred to on the basis of his sexual athleticism and sexual prowess (Poulson-Bryant, 2005).

This deep-seated obsession with black sexuality has led to a distortion of not only the manner in which others see black men but, more importantly, the manner in which some black males view themselves. Here we again see Burglar taking pride in being labelled a 'Mandingo', who is created simply to copulate, and is able to sexually satisfy any female within his immediate vicinity, by virtue alone of being black:

Listen I'm a black man – Mandingo the original, the Alpha, I was made to fuck – ask any amount of women you want to around here.

(Burglar)

This view clearly derives from the psychological inheritance of chattel slavery, where the black male held the same physical and mental status as a domesticated beast; hence common terms for black men such as 'bull', 'buck' or 'stockman', whose primary function was to breed. This can be illustrated by the biological fetishism experienced by British Olympian Linford Christie, who, in the early 1990s, was subjected to unpleasant sexualised and racialised media-led discourses about the dimensions of his 'lunch box' (penis):

Linford Christie is way out in front in every department and we don't just mean the way he stormed to victory in the 100 metres in Barcelona. His

skin tight Lycra shorts hide little as he pounds down the track. His Olym-
pic sized talents are a source of delight for women around the world.

(The Sun, 6 August 1992)

What makes this piece particularly distasteful is the fact that Christie's
achievements in track and field were superlative, as he was (and still is) the
only British sprinter to achieve gold medal status in all four major athletic
competitions.[4] This rekindles Fanon's keen observation about the fascination
of black male genitalia, where the black male is not looked upon as a man but
simply as a phallus:

One is no longer aware of the Negro but only of his penis, the Negro is
eclipsed. He is turned into the penis. He is a penis.

(Fanon, 1967:70)

Black male sexualisation is of key importance within the topic of black masculinities, as, for some men, their physical body may be the only tangible asset
that they feel they hold ownership over, an asset that those such as Burglar
utilise for maximum effect:

The black male defines who he is by the power of his anatomical protrusion, and then further defines the value of what he is by the volume, the
depth, the length and the activity of that anatomical protrusion. As a male,
one is essentially no more than a dangling piece of flesh located about
three inches below the navel.

(Akbar, 1991:23)

Reversing the black masculine stereotype

By living in accordance with principles such as pride, civility, sincerity, and
discretion, these men confirm for themselves, rather than proving to others,
that they possess some of the most important human virtues.

(Duneier, 1992:45)

Attributed traits of black maleness are simply that – attributed. We see black
men struggle to regain some semblance of power by resorting to displays of
machismo, some of which are not necessarily negative or tied to violence. In
Anderson's work (1976, 1999) we notice the primary value that underpins
black life is omitted from mainstream discourses on black men. For Anderson,
the ongoing male pursuit of gaining respect is not inherently tied up within
one male gaining dominion over another. Anderson notes that respect is
obtained by honesty, obligation and responsibility towards family and

associates. For example, 'trouble' is negated by decency, which, according to Anderson, strengthens their peer group position. Therefore, men who frequent 'Jellies'[5] view those who are hardworking, family-orientated and upright in their dealings as individuals worthy of respect.

Liebow (1968) also reinscribes the nature of black maleness, not only in reference to other men but in relation to women. Liebow points out that there are significant traits of black maleness that are often overlooked and/or ignored. Within his study are men who are street tough, but within private and intimate spaces these individuals demonstrate a sensitive slant to their personality, which is consistent with that of a father, breadwinner, husband, lover or son. This was validated in the field, where sample members who hold a high level of street status offered unexpected responses when engaged with in a concealed setting.

Peer-group association is not only concerned with youth, as commonly depicted, but is equally relatable to adult populations. Earlier we saw how Blue describes himself as a 'badman' and an individual not to be crossed. Here he openly declares that he did not learn how to be a man from his father or wider family members. Rather, his adopted mode of maleness was learnt from his peers on the street:

> I was never sat down and taught how to be a man by my dad. I had to learn that shit myself. Runnings on road and those big characters around me taught me all I needed to know in life.
>
> (Blue)

Prominent and influential ethnographies by British scientists have significantly aided our understanding of the dynamics interwoven in the fabric of the peer group in Britain (Downes, 1966; Cohen, 1972; Willis, 1977). However, it is important to keep in mind that the black male peer group has added attachments, as it often acts as a retreat of collective consciousness, when confronted by social rejection and racial prejudice:

> I hung around with both black guys and white guys growing up. We were proper close and looked out for each other. Yeah you could call it my peer group, but when things like race came up it was us black kids that all stuck together. The white guys didn't really have much to say, not in a bad way or anything, I just reckon they couldn't identify with our everyday shit.
>
> (Greenie)

Although speculative suggestions have been made about the nihilistic nature of black peer-group association, this was not apparent in my data. Again it is instructive to keep in the forefront of our minds that black masculinities are not entirely blanketed by negativity, they are laden with more constructive and affirmative traits than is often recognised. Duneier (1992) notes that factors such as respectability, persistence, calmness and application of wisdom are often tied to the peer-group influence amongst adult black men:

> Their images of self worth are not derived from material possessions or the approval of others; they are disciplined ascetics with respect for wisdom and experience; usually humble, they can be quiet, sincere and discreet, and they look for those qualities in their friends.
>
> (Duneier, 1992:163)

Similarly, Liebow (1968) maintains that black masculine traits that are often supported by peer groups are characterised by the male being an attentive father, a kind lover, a breadwinner and a loving son, rather than being solely seen as a social problem:

> By itself, the plain fact of supporting one's wife and children defines the principal obligation of a husband. But the expressive value carried by the providing of this support elevates the husband to manliness.
>
> (Liebow, 1968:131)

Similarly, respondents within my cohort validate the many positive aspects of maleness adopted by black men:

> I will do what I have to do regardless of the consequences, to make sure that my sons are provided for, and provided for well. I don't want my boys having to go through the stuff that I had to go through.
>
> (Greenie)

> I love my wife more than myself – there is nothing that I wouldn't do for her. Whatever she wants, I do my best to provide. Providing is what being a man is all about.
>
> (Mr Gold)

Conclusion

Deliberation surrounding the interconnection of gender, race and age is undoubtedly relevant in academic enquiry related to migrant memoir and rememory, although there is not much British literature germane to it. At times the problems encountered by black men in Britain are explained in reference to the negative depictions of them. Nonetheless, in spite of the continued glut of misrepresentation and offensive pictograms, a small percentage still choose to lean upon and co-opt hyper-, turbo- or uber-masculine traits. Some, such as Gilly, suggest that a black male devoid of machismo and a raw edge is deemed a 'loser', an opinion echoed by Burglar. Key to this is sexualisation, which emerges as a vital factor, as it is here that we notice the cerebral nuances of black men are replaced by wholly physical attributes, leaving any rational essence of the black male to be eclipsed by rumours, anecdotes and gossip that focus upon his penis. The black male becomes the embodiment of sexual excess, appetite and prowess, which establish themselves as signifiers of his manliness, not only for those who view black men but, more worryingly, for some black men themselves.

Nonetheless, despite these hindrances, it can be noted that within private and intimate spaces one can see a reliable and authentic presentation of black manhood. Within these undisclosed spaces, street-tough individuals no longer feel the need to validate themselves by posture and pose. Potent working-class male attributes of breadwinner, provider and protector surface, alongside traits such as calmness, sensitivity and patience.

This chapter points to the small but highly relevant body of ethnographic investigation that shows there are significantly more positive aspects to black adult maleness than is often discussed: a single black masculinity does not exist, but rather various forms of black masculinities, which, like identities, are dictated not just by the subjects themselves but by peripheral issues and broader sociological factors. Whilst I accept that there are black men in Britain who feel disempowered by multiple forms of discrimination and therefore adopt stereotypical behaviour as a coping strategy, or a means to legitimately or illegitimately garner respect, there are those – a greater number – who consciously refuse to embrace such behaviorisms.

Notes

1 Race relations legalisation in Britain had its inception in the 1960s.
2 Compare the 1950s Superman actor to the modern equivalent.
3 The *Terminator* film trilogy.
4 Commonwealth Games, Olympics, European championships and world championships.
5 A corner tavern and liquor store in Southside Chicago where Elijah Anderson carried out ethnographic research.

References

Akbar, N. (1991) *Visions for Black Men*, Tallahassee: Mind Productions.
Alexander, C. E. (1996) 'Black Masculinity', in Owusu, K. (ed.), *Black British Culture & Society: A Text Reader*, London: Routledge, pp. 373–384.
Alexander, C. E. (2001) *The Art of Being Black: The Creation of Black British Youth Identities*, Oxford: Oxford University Press.
Anderson, E. (1976) *A Place on the Corner*, Chicago: The University of Chicago Press.
Anderson, E. (1999) *Code of the Streets: Decency, Violence and the Moral Life of the Inner City*, New York: Norton.

Anderson, E. (2006) 'Jelly's Place: An Ethnographic Memoir', in Hobbs, D. & Wright, R. (eds), *The Sage Handbook of Fieldwork*, Thousand Oaks: Sage, pp. 39–58.

Bowling, B. & Phillips, C. (2002) *Racism, Crime and Justice*, Harlow: Longman.

Cohen, P. (1972) *Sub Cultural Conflict and Working Class Community*, Birmingham: University of Birmingham.

Collingson, M. (1996) 'In Search of the High Life: Drugs, Crime, Masculinity and Consumption', *British Journal of Criminology*, 35(3): 428–444.

Connell, R. W. (1987) *Gender, Power and Society; The Person and Sexual Politics*, Cambridge: Polity Press.

Connell, R. W. (1995) *Masculinities*, Cambridge: Polity Press.

Cooper, C. (2000) 'Virginity Revamped: Representations of Female Sexuality in the Lyrics of Bob Marley and Shabba Ranks', in Owusu, K. (ed.), *Black British Culture & Society: A Text Reader*, London: Routledge, pp. 347–357.

Douglass, F. (1845) *A Narrative of the Life of Frederick Douglass*, Boston: Anti Slavery Office.

Downes, D. (1966) *The Delinquent Solution*, London: Routledge & Kegan Paul.

Du Bois, W. E. B. (1903) *The Souls of Black Folk*, Chicago: A. C. McClurg & Co.

Du Bois, W. E. B. (1907) *The World and Africa: An Inquiry into the Part Which Africa Has Played in World History*, New York: The Viking Press.

Duneier, M. (1992) *Slim's Table: Race, Respectability, and Masculinity*, Chicago: The University of Chicago Press.

Equiano, O. (1998) *The African: The Interesting Narrative of the Life of Olaudah Equiano*, London: The X Press.

Fanon, F. (1967) *Black Skin, White Masks*, New York: Grove Press.

Frazier, E. F. (1940) *The Negro Family in the United States*, Chicago: The University of Chicago Press.

Frazier, E. F. (1963) *The Negro Church in America*, New York: Schocken Books.

Greer, G. (1976) *The Female Eunuch*, London: Paladin.

Gunter, A. (2010) *Growing Up Bad: Black Youth, Road Culture and Badness in an East London Neighbourhood*, London: The Tufnell Press.

hooks, b. (1993) *Black Looks: Race & Representation*, Boston: South End Press.

James, C. L. R. (2001) *The Black Jacobins: Toussaint l'Ouverture & the San Domingo Revolution*, London: Penguin Books.

Katz, J. (2006) *The Macho Paradox: Why Some Men Hurt Women and How All Men Can Help*, Naperville: Sourcebooks.

Kitching, A. (1992) '10 Ways To Pack Your Lunchbox Like Linford'. *The Sun*, 6 August: 15.

Liebow, E. (1968) *Tally's Corner: A Study of Negro Street Corner Men*, Boston: Little Brown.

Majors, R. (1993) *Cool Pose: The Dilemmas of Black Manhood in America*, New York: Touchstone.

Monrose, K. (2016) 'Struggling, Juggling and Street Corner Hustling: The Street Economy of Newham's Black Community', in Antonopoulos, G. (ed.), *Illegal Entrepreneurship, Organized Crime and Social Control, Essays in Honor of Professor Dick Hobbs*, Geneva: Springer, pp. 73–84.

Orbach, S. (2006) *Fat is a Feminist Issue*, London: Arrow Books.

Poulson-Bryant, S. (2005) *Hung: A Meditation on the Measure of Black Men in America*, New York: Doubleday.

Solanas, V. (1968) *S.C.U.M. Manifesto*, New York: Olympia Press.

Welsing, F. C. (1991) *The Isis Papers: The Keys to the Colors*, Chicago: Third World Press.

White, J. (2017) *Urban Music and Entrepreneurship: Beats, Rhymes and Young People's Enterprise*, Abingdon & New York: Routledge.

Willis, P. (1977) *Learning to Labour*, London: Saxon House.

Wykes, M. & Gunter, B. (2004) *If Looks Could Kill*, London: Sage.

Chapter 6

The crisis of the black family in Britain

Black families in Britain are often spoken about in reference to their perceived dysfunction, fractious nature and lack of cohesion (Utting, 2007). The social problems that beleaguer black communities in Britain, such as educational underachievement, through to intra-racial or 'black on black' violence, mean that the effectiveness and structure of black family configuration are often called into question. Lack of stability, father deficit and irresponsible parenting skills are heralded as the main causes of criminality, when discernible within black communities (Ochieng & Hylton, 2010). Whilst I am not convinced by these unsophisticated arguments, I do harmonise with the view that the instability of the black family has an impact on the manner in which they function, West Indian families in particular. It is therefore important to establish the root causes of this destabilisation and subsequent rupture, and address the lack of research in this area (Taylor et al., 1990).

History suggests that the primary cause of the fragmentation of the black family unit has been the transatlantic slave trade; this is incontrovertible. Social historians, sociologists and psychologists (Du Bois, 1903; Fanon, 1963; Akbar, 1991; De Gruy Leary, 2005), who have dared to suggest that the chattel slave trade has significantly contributed to the sociological ills that Diasporised black populations encounter, have often been rebuked and criticised. However, the legacy of the 'Maafa'[1] should never be overlooked. The mere fact that some of the grandfathers of the men interviewed in this book were born into, or subject to, slavery shows just how recent this event was. Therefore the psychosomatic attachment to the slave trade still has much relevance today for a number of reasons. First, the economic infrastructure upon which much of the Americas and Europe have been built is a direct result of the chattel slave trade. Williams (1944) clearly shows that the slave trade funded the Industrial Revolution and the consequent rise of capitalism. Second, and of equal importance, chattel slavery, particularly in Latin America, North America and the Caribbean, was unlike any other form of slavery experienced in world history. Indeed, history teaches us that men have always enslaved other men; but this has often taken the form of intra-racial slave trading that granted basic human and property rights.[2] Limitations of time and space mean that a full exploration of the chattel slave trade cannot be undertaken here; however, a reliable canon of rigorous texts that explore this topic in greater detail is readily available.

Migration from the West Indies to Britain introduced an adaptation in how the black family unit was configured. Because of the abject rural and urban poverty embedded in the post-colonial West Indies, vast numbers of the populace were propelled into economic migration. Most respondents stated that their fathers left their mothers and siblings in the West Indies to travel to 'London', in order to secure employment and make 'big life':

> My parents got here in 1959. My old man left her in Jamaica, and came here to settle down, find work, property and whatever else, and then when that was sorted, send for her to come over.
>
> (Blacker)

Generally speaking, once men secured employment, their wives were sent for, and any children followed at a later date. This undoubtedly had an unsettling effect on those born in the Caribbean, who as children experienced this change in family life. Individuals such as Mr Brown and Mr Gold felt that they lost out on the process of bonding with their parents:

> I'd seen pictures of him, but never met him [his father]. When we met I was told, 'This is your dad'. There was no getting to know him or any-thing, just, 'This is your dad'. That was difficult, and probably why we can't gel and get on to this day.
>
> (Mr Brown)

> I met my dad when I was thirteen. He came to meet me at the airport with a couple of his friends. I still remember that day. They came up to me and said – 'This is your dad!' I still remember thinking that anyone could have come up to me and said that, because I didn't remember seeing any pictures of him, so didn't have a clue what he looked like or who he was.
>
> (Mr Gold)

Unconcealed and everyday forms of racism that were not often witnessed in the Commonwealth territories of the Caribbean were an unpleasant sur-prise for the newly arrived. As noted earlier, accommodation was hard to secure, and employment frequently low-paid and low-status. These factors undoubtedly put huge strains on the newly arrived West Indians as they attempted to adjust to life in their new home. Many who arrived had no desire to stay in Britain for longer than necessary, the sole aim being to accumulate as much wealth as possible within a five-year timeframe.

Retired Faro, who now resides in St Lucia but spent over thirty years in Britain, reflects:

> Well, when I left St. Lucia to come to London it was only for two years, but when I see how things was in London, I had to stay longer.
>
> (Faro)

Faro quickly realised that life in England was tougher than anticipated, and it would take a considerable time to realise his initial economic objectives. Miss Marie (Faro's wife), now in her nineties, recounts:

> I cried a lot at the time. I had to leave my children back home to go to London, and help my husband. He was in England working to make some money to send back for us. It was so hard for him, he needed help. At the time you couldn't travel with children so easily as you wanted to, because you wouldn't be able to get a place to rent, so I had to leave them behind.
>
> (Miss Marie)

As a result of familial fracture, controversial yet significant themes emerge: the disconnect and conflict between sons and fathers, and the thorny issue of corporal punishment within West Indian homes in Britain.

Father versus son: intergenerational conflict and domestic corporal punishment within West Indian homes

> Imagine this, you're fifteen and you've never had a hug, or told 'come here son, I love you – you're the best thing in my life'. The only time you're told you're loved is after you've been beaten.
>
> (Greenie)

The journey to Britain meant that West Indian parents frequently left their children behind to be cared for by extended family members, because, as we have learnt from mothers such as Miss Marie, securing accommodation in Britain for the newly arrived was extremely difficult.

Whilst the Clement Attlee government seemed keen to welcome the 'Sons of the Empire' to Britain for employment, they failed to make adequate provision for housing the newly arrived Commonwealth labour force. The way the Colonial Office addressed such issues was to utilise disused bomb shelters, such as those in Clapham Common, as domiciles. Of course the humiliation of being housed in a subterranean habitat filtered back to the Caribbean, and understandably mothers were reluctant to transport children to Britain. This compromised the familial bonding processes, particularly between fathers and their sons:

To say that African Caribbean fathers and other men are fundamental to the socialisation of children and to an understanding of African Caribbean family life is putting it mildly. That Caribbean men care for their family and provide for them economically has been demonstrated. However, their emotional availability and their social ties to children are unclear.

(Sharpe, 1997:261)

West Indians arrived in Britain possessing strong Victorian and Edwardian moral standards, firmly grounded within the mechanisms of colonialism and religiosity. To be regarded as a well-thought-of and respectable individual, it was of paramount importance to assume the characteristics of Britishness. Regardless of personal privation, fathers stressed the need for their sons to be seen as well brought up, well groomed and neatly attired. Red reflects on the importance of respectability whilst growing up in the West Indies, stating that it was considered shameful for a child to be seen in public with uncombed hair and unkempt garb. Pride in personal appearance was essential:

Back home you had to comb your hair, and have clean fingernails. That was important, and it still applied when we came over here too.

(Red)

British-born Fire adds:

As a youth you couldn't dress like a waste man like some of these youngsters do today, with their trousers sagging around their arse – our parents weren't having it. Look back to the footage of the West Indians coming off of the *Windrush* ship. Look how they dressed in their seamed suits and felt hats, they were a sagaboys [dandies]. My old man always wore a brimmed hat when he left the house. Even if he was only going down the bookies, he always looked respectable and smart.

(Fire)

Similarly, an engagement or conflict with an authority figure, however minimal, was looked upon with scorn and considered a shameful act. Regardless of guilt or innocence, a mere insinuation of wrongdoing was enough to draw wrath. So much so that it was not uncommon for a parent to disown a son for a criminal conviction:

My old man believed all the lies the boy them [police] said about me, so he kicked me out the house and refused to speak to me in public. I was a disgrace to him.

(Burglar)

The same was true in education. For West Indian parents, an educator's assessment of their child was habitually considered right and exact, and schoolteachers were very aware of this, often using this insight to their advantage in an attempt to control black pupil behaviour. A retired schoolteacher explains:

> We didn't have to discipline the West Indian kids too much; all we had to do is tell their parents. That was punishment enough for most of them.
>
> (retired school teacher)

As a result of these factors, a significant number of men are still sensitively disturbed by the lack of emotional support provided by their parents, particularly their fathers:

> My dad was white rum and betting shop man, an old fashioned yardman [Jamaican] you know. Anything that was said about us black boys by a white person he believed them, and we would get beat for it.
>
> (Burglar)

Understandably, this caused distrust, and added to the inevitable consequences of the familial fragmentation caused by migration, with the result that sons found it difficult to communicate rationally with their fathers. Burglar mentions that simple exchanges with parents in the home resulted in terse and indignant responses:

> We couldn't ask any questions in my yard [the home]. When we asked anything we were told shut up or g'way [go away]. It was like my dad was always angry, twenty-four-seven he was vex.
>
> (Burglar)

Blue claimed that his father never taught him any of the rudiments of life, nor how to make his mark in the world as a man:

> My dad was always working – he wasn't a good role model really. He lived at home but was never there. So I had to look to friends and my cousins. You know my dad's not about, so nobody taught me how to be a man.
>
> (Blue)

Blue was not alone in this regard. Fire held similar sentiments:

> My dad never taught me how to do anything. Anything I learnt was from the street and from my mates. My dad came to this country to work, and that was it, he never really learnt anything lasting, or made anything of himself.
>
> (Fire)

This dour assessment of their fathers was clearly significant. For some, though they did not openly hold their fathers in contempt, their feelings of disappointment were clear. Pretty states:

> The men of the *Windrush* era have a lot to answer for. They say they first came here to do this and do that, but the majority of them were just plainly hedonistic. When they first came here all they did was chase white women, party and drink white rum. Years down the line they look at their own youth and criticise them saying that they didn't do anything with what they had built for them, but they themselves didn't build anything in here. They were not like the Irish. The blacks were the help and nothing more. It may not be nice to hear, but it's the truth. Our generation has built a more lasting legacy than they ever did.
>
> (Pretty)

Some suggested that their fathers failed to adequately challenge the racism they encountered on arrival to Britain, and were devoid of any greater aspiration than to simply return to the Caribbean. Mr Brown states:

> The worst racism I experienced, and I've seen a lot of it, was when I left school. My dad was working as a foreman in Stratford, and I used to go in with him sometimes to get some work experience and stuff. There was a two-storey building that was being used as changing rooms. One day I went in there to get changed for work, but the door to the outside was locked, so I used the external steps to get in that way. When I got to the door this white bloke stopped me, and told me that I couldn't go in there because the top floor was for the whites only. This wasn't the Deep South or South Africa, it was Stratford. I went back down and told my dad. He told me that the white bloke was right; we [the blacks] can only use the door downstairs at the back. I said to him, you're in charge here, how can that happen? He never answered me and told me off for asking questions.
>
> (Mr Brown)

These accounts stimulate a debate about the unmentionable and often inviolable topic of domestic discipline, or 'licks', that these men were subject to.[3]

By virtue of West Indian parentage, I am familiar with the term 'licks', but I was not conscious of how much lingering acrimony and bitterness middle-aged men, now fathers and grandfathers, harboured toward the regimes of corporal punishment that they had been subject to in the home. For many, this was the first time they spoke openly about the impact of receiving 'licks', as this is an unmentionable topic within black British communities. Consequently psychological comfort zones and feel-good

factors were ignored, and thus an issue of this magnitude can be scrutinised with the scholarly integrity it deserves:

> Black people, as a collective are becoming increasingly sophisticated. We
> are becoming strong enough to face many unpleasant realities and truths
> about ourselves, and the social site, and world that we live in, without denial
> or panic. The ability to analyze ourselves, our behaviour, and our reality cru-
> cially is one of the signs of true mental health. Another equally important
> aspect of mental health is our full acceptance of the responsibility for
> reorganizing our own behaviour in order to change things that are wrong.
>
> (Welsing, 1991:230)

Within the milieu of academic research into the black condition, Welsing's
postulation is sound. My research identified a pattern of aggression within
West Indian homes in Britain, defined as 'discipline', that is absent from the
relatively sparse sociological literature on black British family life. Those
interviewed freely used terms such as 'violence', 'abuse' and 'cruelty' when
recounting the manner in which 'licks' were administered. Interestingly, however, this candour was often relayed with an accompanying air of jest, or
a hint of joviality. Nonetheless, once probed, the true ramifications of receiving
'licks' and the accepted normality of the practice, revealed the serious harm it
did to the maintenance and cohesive functioning of familial relationships:

> Being beaten was a rite of passage for all of us black boys home or
> abroad. It's something that we don't even talk about much, because it's
> a given that all of us had experienced it.
>
> (Pretty)

The uncomfortable smiles that rode in tandem with memoirs of receiving
'licks' went a little way to convince me that those who were on the receiving
end of the 'strap' considered such floggings warranted and unjustified:

> Ken, I used to get beat for everything. I remember once when fifteen, my
> mum was giving me earache, and kept going on and on. I just got up and
> said 'choops' [kissing his teeth]. Who told me to do that? As I was
> making my way downstairs and saw her coming up with a kettle in her
> hand. I thought, 'What's she doing with a kettle?' She threw the kettle of
> boiling water on me.
>
> (Fat Larry)

He continues:

> I reckon my parents didn't know any better. That's what they learnt and
> had to put up with, so over time they just did what they thought was best

for their kids. I suppose they thought that that was the right thing to do. If life is about giving your kids better than what was given to you, I dread to think what growing up was like for them.

(Fat Larry)

Fat Larry poses a valid question that helps construct a usable framework for investigating this matter further. It seems clear that a number of parents who were raised in the post-colonial Caribbean were themselves victims of physical violence as children, and merely perpetuated such behaviour. This highlights two fundamental factors. First, notions of violence are deeply ingrained within the psyche of Caribbean people, and second, as is pointed out by Wilson (1993), these acts of violence are often hackneyed, simulated and then disseminated. A question then arises: where does a behaviour originate that is seemingly ingrained within the collective consciousness of some West Indian populations? This question can be addressed by means of a slight but nonetheless relevant reflective detour.

Historical accounts inform us that various forms of violence were used as methods of control within the machinery of chattel enslavement. In order to secure compliance, the enslaved were physically beaten into submission, as to break their will and curb any disobedience or defiance. It is well known that upon arrival at the staging posts or sugar plantations in the Caribbean, the bondsmen were 'broken in' – forced to be acquiescent and yielding. In time, these methods were instilled in the enslaved themselves, who went on to perpetuate them on each other. C. L. R. James mentions:

[T] here was no ingenuity that fear or a depraved imagination could devise which was not employed to break their spirit and satisfy the lusts and resentment of their owners and guardians – irons on the hands and feet, blocks of wood that the slaves had to drag behind them wherever they went, the tin-plate mask designed to prevent the slaves eating sugar-cane, the iron collar. Whipping was interrupted in order to pass a piece of hot wood on the buttocks of the victim; salt, pepper, citron, cinders, aloes and hot ashes were poured on the bleeding wounds. Mutilations were common, limbs, ears, and sometimes the private parts, to deprive them of the pleasures which they could indulge in without expense. Their masters poured burning wax on their arms and hands and shoulders, emptied boiling sugar cane over their heads, burned them alive, roasted them on slow fires, filled them with gunpowder and blew them up with a match: buried them up to the neck and smeared their heads with sugar that flies might devour them; fastened them near to nests of ants or wasps; made them eat their excrement, drink their urine, and lick the saliva of other slaves.

(James, 2001:10)

One can therefore deduce that the shape of the domestically administered corporal punishment experienced by the post-*Windrush* generation indeed showed outlines of practices copied from colonisers. Clearly respondents did not experience the excessive forms of ill-treatment outlined above, but they maintain in their own words that they were subject to questionable regimes of punishment at home. Without doubt the term 'abuse', particularly in reference to power relationships between child and adult, is acerbic and inexcusable, but, according to some respondents, abuse is what it was:

> Of course it was abuse, what else was it if it wasn't abuse? No matter how black people want to dress it up and deny it, it was abuse.
>
> (Mr Gold)

A number of men claimed they were not simply spanked with an open hand or, in British working-class parlance, 'got a clip round the ear', they received 'licks', and unyieldingly maintained that they were victims of physical abuse. Rambo selects this experience of growing up in rural Jamaica:

> Dem did tie me up to an old chair with a piece a rope. Then dash a tin condensed milk pon me star. Remember me outside inna di sun, and it did hot – I couldn't move. You know what that do? The milk attract the red ants them, and the ants dem bite mi you know man – pure wickedness.
>
> (Rambo)

As torturous as Rambo's experience undoubtedly was, an overwhelming number of respondents claimed that 'licks' did them no harm. However, when asked if they, as parents now, would use the same level of discipline on their children, they all resoundingly said no. Interestingly, as a child Red believed that 'licks' were an experience reserved only for those born in the West Indies. He confessed that in Antigua it was widely believed that British-born blacks were free from receiving 'licks':

> In the Antigua we were told that if you lived in England you didn't get licks. I couldn't wait to get to England, but when I arrived I was surprised to see that my cousins who were born there got licks too – I was shocked.
>
> (Red)

It is of interest that there was a distinct division between those born in the West Indies and those born in Britain in the way discipline was discussed. Those born in the West Indies spoke of discipline in a humourless and unsmiling manner. For them 'licks' was serious business, and not something to be taken lightly. Expressions whilst recounting the beatings exposed feelings of soreness, resentment and deep-seated injustice, adding a further layer to an already complex narrative, as many of those of who were born in the

Caribbean were not brought up by their biological parents, because of migration. This meant discipline was managed arbitrarily, often by extended family members, teachers, religious elders or care providers. Conversely those born in Britain often adopted a humorous and jocular attitude to receiving licks:

> When I look back to the funniest times of growing up it was when we used to get beat. My friend's mum used to beat him and we would all be outside his house bending up with laughter. Boy, Ken, it was funny like that. Even today I know some men who get beaten in front of their own children. Imagine, 'Daddy, why is Granddad beating you with his belt?' That's fucked up.
>
> (Fire)

So, the scrutiny of the social scientist remains and ponders: what were the long-term results of receiving 'licks'? It seems that 'licks' can prove to be both positive and negative, simply depending on the individual. Fat Larry, for example, believed that the 'licks' he endured encouraged a rebellious spirit to emerge that led him to shun any form of authority, be it parent, educator or law enforcer:

> [I got beaten] with anything. Whatever my old man or old dear got their hands on. The belt buckle was their favorite. The way I carried on [in reference to crime], was a way of me dealing with my frustrations. I had to get this anger out of me, and the only way I knew how to do it was to go out there and be a fucking nuisance.
>
> (Fat Larry)

On the other hand, despite suggesting that 'licks' in his experience were mean-spirited, Nev retrospectively believes that they benefited him in the long run as an adult:

> If it wasn't for the licks I got as a child I'd probably be in the jailhouse today. A good set of licks is what these youths need today to keep them in line. I'm not saying to abuse them, but bend the tree when it's young, or as the scriptures say, 'Spare the rod and spoil the child'.
>
> (Nev)

Undoubtedly this is a very contentious area of debate, and some academics with whom I shared my research intentions suggested I avoid it at all costs. But since it was such a protruding theme, I simply had to tackle it squarely. I envisage that some will conclude that West Indian parents habitually physically abuse their children, and it is clear that some respondents such as Rambo and Fat Larry, who were on the receiving end of extreme forms of discipline, might agree, but personally this is not a view I hold fast to. Finally, it is also worth mentioning that the threat of, or actual, physical beating did not only take place domestically. Those who were schooled in the West Indies made clear that fear of receiving 'licks' within the classroom was ever present:

> The thought of the teachers and their long brown thick leather straps made me quiver. I felt the strap a number of times, but not the long skinny cane. Each time I was asked a question in class I would stand and tremble, because all the time I could imagine the pain of the strap on my back. The speed and the force with which the teacher brought it down on the other boys' backs would make me fear being in their position. The pain and agony.
>
> (O'Connor, 1979:22)

I will speak more on the educational regimes that black men in Britain were subject to in the next chapter.

Conclusion

This chapter is of crucial significance as it provides a privileged insight into some of the most potent but muted experiences in the lives of black men in Britain. The machinery of the family acts as an indicator to gauge identity and gender formation, as this is the site where socialisation begins. The first point to establish here is that, historically, the shape and structure of the black family unit has transformed at various junctures, in an attempt to cope with the broader social factors to which it has been subject.

All the respondents mentioned the numerous challenges their families faced whilst they grew up, and how these childhood experiences acted as key components in shaping their current lives as sons, fathers and husbands. Their narratives dispel stereotypical representations of the nature of black family life, such as the absent-father paradigms, and show that, although sometimes fragmented, and different in structure to the typical British (white) family unit, black families still thrive and remain functional within their perceived dysfunction. The testimonies of the men within this chapter should be commended for their frankness and honesty, as they prove that the post-*Windrush* generation is willing to engage in topics previous black British generations have ignored for fear of recrimination. Addressing this scholarly omission provides an alternative understanding of black British family life, which is valuable in unravelling the muted legacy of violence ingrained in West Indian culture.

What is important in the final analysis is the significance of the broader historical and sociological context. The legacy of the chattel slave trade throughout the African Diaspora is still very evident. Some suggest black people ought to move on, and refrain from any reflective analysis of these events, as it is no longer relevant or was a 'long time ago'. However, the minds of those making such assertions should be reminded that the grandparents and great-grandparents of a sizable number of the post-*Windrush* generation (who are now grandparents themselves) were born, or were alive, before the time the slave trade was officially abolished in the West Indian territories. This is not long ago, and it is still highly relevant in many fields of academic enquiry pertaining to African Diasporised populations.

Black family life in Britain is often defined in reference to its unconventional configuration. The focus on father deficit and families headed by unmarried females often dominates discourses on black family life. The stale dish of poor parenting is constantly re-served as the cause of any social ills within black communities, but the truth is more substantial than these narrow views. My data collection countered such assumptions. For example, of all sample members who were British-born, only one was raised in a single-parented family, and none of the men born in the West Indies were from single-parented families. Moreover, only a small number of sample members raised in dual-parented households, who are now fathers themselves, are unmarried or estranged from the mothers of their children. This disproves insinuations of widespread father deficit amongst the post-*Windrush* generation. Although rifts between fathers and sons undoubtedly existed, fathers were still very much loved and respected, and featured heavily in their sons' lives.

Notes

1 Swahili for 'great destruction' or The Black Holocaust.
2 E.g. the Hebrew Israelites' enslavement by the Egyptians as outlined in the Torah, or servitude in Slavic regions of Europe.
3 Corporal punishment or being beaten/physically disciplined.

References

Akbar, N. (1991) *Visions for Black Men*, Tallahassee: Mind Productions.
De Gruy Leary, J. (2005) *Post Traumatic Slave Syndrome: America's Legacy of Enduring Injury and Healing*, Milwaukee: Uptone Press.
Du Bois, W. E. B. (1903) *The Souls of Black Folk*, Chicago: A. C. McClurg & Co.
Fanon, F. (1963) *The Wretched of the Earth*, New York: Grove Press.
James, C. L. R. (2001) *The Black Jacobins: Toussaint l'Ouverture and the San Domingo Revolution*, London: Penguin Books.
O'Connor, E. (1979) *Our Lives: Young Peoples' Autobiographies*, London: The Inner London Education Authority English Centre.
Ochieng, B. & Hylton, C. (2010) *Black Families in Britain as the Site of Struggle*, Manchester: Manchester University Press.
Sharpe, J. (1997) 'Mental Health Issues and Family Socialisation in the Caribbean', in Roopnarine, J. L. & Brown, J. (eds), *Caribbean Families: Diversity among Ethnic Groups*, Greenwich: Ablex, pp. 259–273.
Taylor, R., Chatters, L., Tucker, M. & Lewis, E. (1990) 'Developments in Research on Black Families: A Decade Review', *Journal of Marriage and the Family*, 78(4): 340–351.

Utting, D. (2007) *Parenting & the Different Ways It Can Affect Children's Lives: Research Evidence*, London: Joseph Roundtree Foundation.

Welsing, F. C. (1991) *The Isis Papers: The Keys to the Colors*, Chicago: Third World Press.

Williams, E. (1944) *Capitalism and Slavery*, Chapel Hill: University of North Carolina Press.

Wilson, A. N. (1993) *The Falsification of Afrikan Consciousness: Eurocentric History, Psychiatry and the Politics of White Supremacy*, New York: Afrikan World Info Systems.

Chapter 7

Uneducated, educated or mis-educated?

The disabling nature of racism within the British educational system is not something that can be easily peroxided and pomaded for the sake of appearance, as has often been tried. It remains an awkward topic, particularly in reference to the post-*Windrush* generation. In this chapter I will examine the challenges that these men as children faced within the British educational system, and the impact of these challenges on their eventual life chances and life courses. I will begin, however, by looking at the significance of social class within British education, and how this often dictates school governance, and social reproduction. This is vital if we keep in mind the absence of a visible structure of social class in black British populations, where we see race perpetually override social position.

Race and class

At the core of inequalities in Britain lies the class structure (Preston, 2007). Nowhere is this more apparent than within the educational system (Drew, 1995). The regimes that exist within institutions of education mirror broader issues of social class, cultural capital and division of labour. Bowles and Gintis (1976) suggest that schools that accommodate working-class students are often hidebound, disciplined and authoritarian, whereas institutions of education intended for the middle-class hierarchy and above are frequently less restrictive and more democratic.

For the black student, the lack of an appropriate embodied disposition or *habitus* (Bourdieu, 1984, 1988) arguably lies at the root of the troubled relationship with British education. Moreover, observers such as Althusser (1971) view a student possessing a fitting mode of cultural capital as an absolute necessity for success within a capitalist economy. Members of the post-*Windrush* generation were frequently unable to obtain the cultural capital necessary to successfully navigate educational regimes, lacking the required *hexis*, such as linguistic code, accent and consumption pattern. This deficiency placed them at an immediate disadvantage within systems of education at all levels.

By the 1970s, the assimilation of black students into British education was not as effortless as first assumed. Due to the aforesaid issues of cultural capital and reproduction, black students, particularly those born in the West Indies, were disproportionately written off as 'educationally sub-normal'. Labelling such as this, highlighted by Coard (1971), exposed the shameful modes of governance that existed in schools regarding the treatment of black children, and questioned the models of assimilation fixed within the British educational system. The early 1980s saw a shift from the sculpt of assimilation towards a model of integration within some ethnically and racially diverse schools. Integration supposedly meant that open-mindedness, and cultural tolerance towards the needs of non-white students, would be adopted, in order to improve educational attainment levels (Mullard, 1982). Instead, like assimilation, the model possessed significant flaws. As we will see later, this prompted an almost quasi-essentialist position, which encouraged black students to focus on lifestyle, sport and music rather than life chances, life skills and academic excellence.

The post-*Windrush* generation, who undertook their schooling at arguably the most significant timeframe in British history in respect of race and education, were subject to both of these experimental educational processes.

The parents of these students, many of whom were from backgrounds of peasantry and raised in the harshness of post-colonial Caribbean paucity, saw an English education as a means by which their children could escape the biting poverty they had to endure:

> The money you take and go to the pub with, use it and send your children to university. In a few years time your son will be walking and a white will be carrying his stool. Don't aim for the job that you have to beg for, aim for the job that they beg you to do. For God's sake give your child a good education.
>
> (Pryce, 1979:198)

The reality, however, was somewhat different from this idealistic flight of fancy.

Very few of the men I spoke to had a positive experience in their years of compulsory education. Violence, racial abuse, exclusion and disenchantment were recurring themes. Overwhelmingly those interviewed saw their educators as part of a tempestuous 'us and them' relationship, like with politicians and police, or, as defined by Fanon, as a relationship between the coloniser and the 'other' (Fanon, 1967). The lasting perception of the British educational system for the post-*Windrush* generation was of yet another public institution that existed to oppress, fragment and subjugate. What becomes clear is that, for those in this study, the playgrounds, school halls and classrooms acted as forums where instances of confrontation, discrimination and prejudice were frequently played out:

The obstacles confronting the West Indian child in the British classroom are tremendous, and are the chief cause of the notoriously slow progress he makes. Mainly because of his mutilating colonial heritage, the West Indian child is severely handicapped and cannot make the tremendous adjustment necessary to remedy the deficits in his socio-cultural background, which he must do if he is to take full advantage of the educational opportunities open to him in his new metropolitan environment. It is unrealistic to think, for example, that unaided – without sympathy, compassion and the provision of extra special facilities to facilitate the transaction – the young West Indian can overcome all short comings of his inferior educational upbringing and colonial origin, and suddenly respond to the considerably different and more difficult demands made on him by the British school system.

(Pryce, 1979:120)

A good British education

The crisis within British education for the men in this study began in the early 1970s, when, as the children of immigrants, they entered British schools. Some had already begun their education in the Caribbean, so the change of regime understandably shook them. Oakley (1968) clearly identifies the established methods of education within Caribbean schools:

Teaching methods are, on the whole not far removed from those in England a century ago . . . With large classes in little space, and few books or materials for active learning, children are early drilled into sitting still and keeping quiet. The strap or the stick is in frequent use and, although punishment is not as harsh as they were formerly, in some schools they are very severe. Parental discipline is on the same lines, and parents expect a good teacher to beat him well and make him learn good.

(Oakley, 1968:17)

One of the themes commonly mentioned by those born in the West Indies concerned the greater level of discipline and propriety within the schools they attended in the Caribbean before coming to Britain, particularly in reference to attire and appearance:

You had to be neat and clean, when you were going to school. That was very important.

(Mr Brown)

Appearance was important. We used to line up and have to show our nails, and if they were dirty, we'd get hit with a ruler. It used to keep you on your toes. They'd get a pencil and put it through your hair, and if it didn't go through easily then they would know that your hair is not combed – that was normal.

(Red)

These comments can be attested to by the general aspiration of respectability that existed (and still exists) amongst both the poor urban and rural peasant class communities of the West Indies (Monrose, 2017). High ideals in attire, correctness and decency were instilled from an early age, and teachers were considered purveyors of these qualities; teachers in the Caribbean were held in the same esteem as parents, pastors or priests, and children learned not to question their authority:

You would get whipped at school, and the thing was you couldn't go home and tell your parents that you got whipped in school, because from they hear that you'd get another beating.

(Red)

Pretty was born in Britain, and completed his primary and early secondary education in East London. When he was fifteen his parents decided to return to Jamaica to pursue their business interests. As a result, Pretty undertook the latter part of his secondary education in Jamaica, and returned to England in his early twenties. He is ideally positioned to compare West Indian and British systems of education, having experienced both:

When I went to Jamaica at fifteen, I had to retake my fifth form. I did local examinations, and passed those, but I knew that Jamaican diplomas were not going to be of any use to me when I came back to the UK. So I went to community college and did a year of six subjects at 'O' level, and then two years at 'A' level. It was a lot to take in, but had I still been in England I don't think I would have got them, because there was too much distraction. By that I don't mean only friends and that sort of stuff, but all of the social issues that black people had to deal with.

(Pretty)

Although impressed with the Caribbean standard of education, Pretty found that the certification awarded in Jamaica did not hold the same kudus as those awarded in Britain. Therefore, before returning to the UK, he thought it necessary to be armed with a glut of academic qualifications in order to compete productively within the British job market:

Although I was English, my qualifications were Jamaican, so I needed to be qualified over and above the normal English candidate.

(Pretty)

Respondents were often high-spirited and enthusiastic whilst recounting their schooling years in the Caribbean. Due to the climate, schooling took place outside, and not by being 'in a prison', as Mr Brown described his school in England. Although the fear of being disciplined by 'the strap' was ever present for the most trivial of misdemeanours, this was displaced by the freedom and openness of West Indian school life. Full-time education for those born in the West Indies seemed a significantly happier experience than that of their British-born counterparts, who noted that British pupils' attitude to education was dispassionate and nonchalant, compared to the more competitive approach of West Indian schooled students:

> In my experience, English black students didn't have that much ambition, nor did they have much drive when it came to education. If they were gifted in a particular area they did well. It wasn't a case of working hard at anything. In Jamaica you have to pay for your education. Jamaica is a developing country, so money isn't easy to come by. Parents spend a lot of money sending their children to school, so there is an expectation that the students make the most of the opportunity, so kids were very studious. In class if you didn't get good grades, your friends would mock you and call you 'dunce head' and ask you to stop messing around because they didn't want your ignorance to rub off on them. Whereas in England if your grades were bad and you didn't pay attention at the school, your friends gave you a pat on the back.
>
> (Pretty)

Joining a new school meant that this was also the first time close interaction with those from other races occurred. Indeed, Europeans and Asians had been seen in the West Indies, but never in the same context as in an English classroom. Mr Gold mentioned that 'back home' he never saw white people walking on the street; they rode in cars, lived in big palatial homes and went to different schools. As a child in St Lucia he believed all white people were wealthy. Upon arrival in London, however, he was shocked to see white people who were poor:

> The whites that lived in St Lucia had the best jobs, the best houses, had cars and owned shops. It was strange seeing that then coming to London and seeing poor white people, because I had never seen a poor white person. I had never seen a white person sitting in the street, or drunk until then, and it was a real shock to the system.
>
> (Mr Gold)

Similarly, Mr Brown's first real experience of racial difference occurred on his way to Britain:

> I came over on a boat and not a like most people who came on a plane. It was my first contact with a lot of white people. I remember them telling

me I can't go upstairs on the upper deck, and it confused me. I was a kid and was used to being free and doing what I wanted. It wasn't until later that I got to understand that the whites rode on the top deck, and the blacks had to stay in the bottom of the boat.

(Mr Brown)

Once in school, the West Indian migrant children were quickly introduced to the challenges of not only race but ethnicity and cultural identity. For example, the difficulties in communicating with their black classmates:

I went to secondary school at thirteen soon after I arrived from St Lucia. I was an outsider, because although there were other black kids like me, they were English, which I thought was weird. My first friend, a guy called Michael Gordon, was from Dominica but had adapted well, and took me under his wing. He showed me the ropes, and I clung onto him. There were things that were being said that I couldn't really understand, because words had different meanings.

(Mr Gold)

The challenges facing West Indian children settled in Britain were not given direct investigation by educational administrators at the time. However, commentators such as Coard (1971) and Oakley (1968) noticed this lack. The conclusions reached suggested that the cultural dislocation experienced by these youngsters was of major significance, and had a direct effect on both their mental health and their academic development. Coard (1971) points out that the 'educationally subnormal' (ESN) label affixed upon a large number of black schoolchildren in the 1970s was in fact a direct response to cultural and racial indifference on the part of the British education system. If black students failed to successfully negotiate the cultural difficulties that were in place within the school, they were deemed to be less able than other students. Fire speaks candidly of his experience of British schooling upon his arrival from St Kitts. He states that all the pupils in his class were black, or 'of colour', which, he perceived, was the reason why his class was ranked as the 'bottom group and full of low achievers':

I was in the bottom class for every subject at school, apart from PE [physical education], and that's because in PE wasn't graded. In my year the top players at football, rugby and cricket were always black, but they never let a black guy be captain of any of the teams. In things like maths, English and science, they'd put all the bad kids, who always seemed to be black, or shall I say non-white, in the same class with the worst fucking teachers who didn't have rarse clue of how to teach. What sense is that? If we are the worst pupils, give us the best teachers so we can learn something.

(Fire)

As Fire also mentions, the issue of sport participation within schooling deserves scrutiny, as it seems the sporting prowess of black pupils frequently took precedence over their academic achievement. Blacks were overrepresented within the school sports teams, and under-represented in supplementary school subjects such as English literature and languages. What is also of interest is that although blacks were over-represented in school sports teams, very few were given the responsibility of being team captain. This was reserved for their white teammates, again an observable fact, spoken of in greater detail by King (2000). In the subsequent section I will pay particular attention to the sport of football, as this was a pastime most of those interviewed held an affinity with during school years, and seemed eager to talk about.

Football crazy – football mad: the black student and sport

Sample members overwhelmingly highlighted football, more than boxing, cricket or track and field, as being their most popular leisure activity whilst growing up. A significant number of men interviewed could effortlessly recount an anecdote involving football without much prompting. Whether it surrounded the hero worship of a specific player or team, or being a spectator, football for this generation of men, unlike anything else, acted as something greater than a passport to tie them to Britishness. For many, football was an equaliser, and provided an opportunity to shed the shackles of racial discrimination. Akin to white working-class male adolescents, many aspired from a young age to be professional footballers, and retrospectively perceived football as one of the few positive arenas in which both black and white working-class males could excel (Willis, 1977; King, 2000). When asked about role models and heroes of their youth, respondents offered footballers such as Pele, Nobby Stiles, Frank Worthington and Clyde and George Best. Race did not seem to be an issue within the fantasy football world of black teenagers in Britain. For them, if you were good enough, then you were good enough to make the team. Some were undoubtedly gifted, and went on to be considered for trials with professional clubs such as Millwall and Tottenham. None, however, within my sample made the mark and turned professional, although many from Newham did, such as Liburd Henry, Sol Campbell, Alex Dyer, and Jermain Defoe. Nonetheless, what did emerge, and is not often spoken about, is that those who clearly possessed a talent for sport were often discouraged from pursuing their dreams of becoming professional sportsmen by their parents, who did not see a career in sports as a viable employment option. Greenie, now a manager of an adult entertainment holding, states that his mother dictated his employment options, and being a footballer was not part of her selection:

My mum used to say, 'Footballer? My son has to be a computer engineer, and then has to and go and work in a bank.' I was like 'Wow mum you've got big plans for me'. Who would think I would go on to manage a strip club after that. Well at least I get footballers visiting the club.

(Greenie)

A lack of enthusiasm and support on the part of parents for their sons' pathway in sport is a recurring theme. Respondents noticed that the parents of white team members would often attend matches and participate in the running of football teams, whether in coaching, management or administration. However, black parents rarely participated in or even attended football games:

It helps if your old man got involved in the running of the team. Some of the white boys who shouldn't have even got picked to play in the team did, only because their dad used to drink with the team manager.

(Jay)

Due to the demands of their employment, parents possibly did not prioritise sport attendance as either worthwhile or welcoming. Soccer during the 1970s and 1980s was only just beginning to accommodate and integrate blacks as part of the game. Moreover, football grounds at this time were notorious for overt displays of nationalism and racism, which meant black attendance was somewhat of a rarity (Back et al., 2001; Garland, 2001). The outcome was that gifted black players felt increasingly isolated, as they failed to secure the same level of support from their families as their teammates: support that was often necessary to succeed at the highest level of a very competitive and enormously selective profession:

I got picked to play for Essex, which at my age was a big deal. I was a lot younger than the other boys in the team – that showed how good I was. I remember being on the coach suited and booted, all official like, travelling to play somewhere up North miles away. I was only fourteen, and looked around me, and saw these white boys with their dads and stuff, but I was all alone – the star player on his own. I just thought to myself I didn't want this, I'd rather be on the estate playing cannons or knockout Wembley with my mates.

(Jay)

Parental expectation placed a huge pressure on sons, as they felt obligated to make career choices aimed at satisfying their parents, whose well-worn testaments regarding the sacrifices they had made for them became etched upon their psyche. This prompted respondents to believe that parents were adding to the constrained opportunities for second-generation blacks in Britain:

When I was younger I wanted to join the army, or be a professional footballer. I was always interested in sport. Take me out the classroom, put me on the sports field, and I was happy, but my dad said no, I shouldn't look to sport; I should do 'this or that' instead, without telling me what 'this or that' was.

(Fat Larry)

The quest for acceptance, and to be seen as respectable at any cost, meant that parents failed to adequately appraise the range of skills their children possessed. Mr Gold and Fat Larry, like Greenie, indicate the belief that West Indian parents wanted children to be what they wanted them to be, without any encouragement, prior consultation or say in the decision-making process:

You know they wanted to make me into what they wanted me to be without even getting to know me, or what I was good at.

(Mr Gold)

The white elephant in the classroom: racism within school governance

The *Windrush* arrivals were clearly unaware of the carnage and destruction that an often poisonous British educational system had in store for their children. The legacy of this would be seen some years later:

The level of the blatant racist abuse that some of the teachers gave us was incredible. They would call us 'nigger' and 'Black Bastard' and all kinds of stuff. It became normal at school. 'Go on get over there you Black Bastard'. 'Shut your black lips when you look at me'. 'Come on, Golly – hurry up'. Even got us to read some of those racist Enid Blyton books as part of the courses. Our parents didn't know what we went through, and what was the point of telling them? They'd never believe us.

(Fire)

As previously noted, those born in the West Indies who came to Britain as teenagers during the 1960s and 1970s were not usually accustomed to dealing with issues of race. Seemingly overnight, however, their lives moved from monochrome to Technicolor. Moreover, they had also shifted from being part of the majority to being part of a minority. The British-born men, however, knew about racism, and were well acquainted with how it operated within an everyday context, particularly at school.

Established culture, regimes and attitudes within the classroom soured the experience of school for some, and in some instances led to the development of delinquent patterns of behaviour. Blacker firmly places his exclusion and subsequent expulsion from education in the lap of teachers who he believed failed him:

> I asked questions at school, but got no answers. They kicked me out of school because they couldn't deal with my curiosity. When I was thirteen my older brother turned Rasta, and told me to ask my teachers questions about black history. Believe me, Ken, the next day I was excited and I couldn't wait to ask them, but they couldn't answer me. I was a curious youth so I pressed and pressed until my teacher said, 'Stop pressuring me with your questions. Get out my class!' That was the kind of attitude that I rebelled against. She should have told me to go to the library to look it up or something constructive, but instead just kicked me out.
>
> (Blacker)

Teachers' perceived lack of interest in black students was similarly felt by Fat Larry:

> As I said the school didn't really care about us as black kids, that's the way it felt anyway. Nobody asked us any questions. Nobody took an interest in us or our culture, and why should they.
>
> (Fat Larry)

Gillborn (1995) offers some insight into this by offering what is known as 'the myth of black challenge', which often manifests itself within multiracial schools in low-income areas. Black – typically Afro Caribbean – students are considered a challenge for educators, which prompts a disproportionate amount of punishment and criticism to be levelled at them. In the case of Blacker, this meant eventual expulsion, not necessarily on the basis of misbehaviour but due to poor pupil/teacher engagement and interaction. Established pedagogical practice suggests that if a student questions a teacher, and challenges the existing paradigms on a topic, perhaps with an alternative viewpoint, typically this is seen as positive and commendable, since it develops critical thinking. However, according to Gillborn, when instances such as these involve black students, the educator finds it disruptive to the teaching process, thus rendering the student a 'troublemaker'. Gillborn further suggests that teachers often encourage and embrace students who are identified as being 'ideal clients', or 'teachable'. These students, it is suggested, are typically white, or Asian.

The majority of the men stated their biggest problem within their schools was their perception of racism. Racism for them was sometimes overtly presented, but more often subtle and understated. According to Blue, teachers' low expectation of black students was self-evident:

> Teachers thought they could overstep the mark, and I wasn't having it. White people in general like to try that shit. With teachers I found that if

you let them take liberties with you once, then they do it all the time. So I'd always nip it in the bud. I remember a teacher who'd say things like 'You're going to end up dead or in jail you will,' or say sarcastic things like 'You'll be a dancer when you're older,' shit like that. As a child you're naive as to how the world sees you as a black person and laugh along. Trust me anywhere I see that teacher now as old as he might be, I'd give him a life changing beating.

(Blue)

Fire had similar experiences:

Teachers said I was rubbish. All the guys I hung around with were told the same thing as me. Papers, television, books, comics, police – whatever, they all said you were rubbish – so what do you end up thinking?

(Fire)

Low self-esteem, poor self-image and lack of self-belief were inevitable consequences of the lazy teaching methods and blatant racial prejudice displayed by some of the teachers respondents encountered. Clearly no shared aims or commonality past sport participation existed upon which a teacher/student relationship could be established and maintained. Fat Larry shockingly described how the mode of dress adopted by some teachers was clearly offensive and encouraged confrontation:

My school was shit so we had a load of fill-in teachers because of the violence inside and outside the place. They had this one particular teacher come to the school dressed like a skinhead. Braces, bleached jeans with turn ups in them, and red eighteen hole Dr Marten boots. Ken, we fucked him up proper, even the white kids jumped in. The man was a complete cunt! You can't come to teach in Manor Park looking like you're NF [National Front member] in a school full of blacks – that's taking the piss.

(Fat Larry)

Whilst the political views of teachers were not often so openly displayed in the classroom, as in the case of the supposed National Front teacher that Fat Larry speaks of, the same cannot be said of school governance and local education authority administration:

The local authority also saw black children as a threat to the social cohesion of the school (they could only be integrated in small numbers), and this was further reinforced by the corralling of black children into special schemes: withdrawal classes for Asian children with language difficulties, and schools for the educationally subnormal (ESN) for Afro Caribbean children perceived to have behavioural problems.

(Newham Monitoring Project, 1991:24)

This typifies the regimes at the heart of education management throughout Newham in the 1970s and 1980s. As the demography of the borough began to shift with the increased influx of black and Asian families, the LEA could no longer sustain the restricted entry of black students into its flagship (overwhelmingly white) schools. In order to deflect any accusations of racial discrimination, black students were now permitted entry into these more 'prestigious' schools. However, this decision proved unpopular among a number of white teachers, who, it is alleged, were unhappy about 'having' to teach an increased number of 'foreigners'. As a result, a significant number left their posts within the borough. This had dire consequences for both the administrative reputation of the schools in question and the education of the pupils concerned. Seemingly overnight, previously high-ranking schools became failing institutions, because they simply could not attract and retain 'good teachers', because 'good teachers' would prefer not to teach black students (I have first-hand experience of this as a lecturer, in previous positions, where some staff have openly disclosed their fearful apprehension at supervising black students, or teaching on modules with a large cohort of black students). Contentiously, as is well known, local education authorities and council legislators in boroughs such as Newham at the time, despite their prejudiced and discriminatory operations, were not held accountable. This, like the ongoing debates on educational underachievement of black male students and white working-class male students, apportions blame to all aside from those in educational administration and governance.

As touched upon in the foregoing chapter, some respondents spoke of the ruptured relationship between themselves and their parents. Parents had a set career path devised that they expected their offspring to follow. However, substandard teaching techniques, and veiled, and sometimes not so veiled, racial prejudice in schools, meant that many sons left school less academically equipped than their parents would have assumed. This had a negative impact on the parent/child relationship, and added to the increasing difficulties black males were to face upon entering manhood:

> All decisions were taken out my hands. You remember when you left primary school, and they asked you what high school you wanted to go to, and you would say I want to go to this one or that one? Well I never had that option. From early I was told it was like this. 'This is where you're going and these are the subjects you will do – end of story'. There was a fairly scary element in the way that that was done.

(Greenie)

A regrettable truth is that racism in its various guises has been a key component in the lives of British black men. What makes this even more unfortunate is that it is in the realm of education where the experience of racial prejudice is most commonly mentioned. This should not come as too much of a surprise, because, as we have seen in Chapter 2, institutions of intellectualism (education) are where racial stereotypes are birthed and gain validation (Isaac, 2001).

State-endorsed investigations surrounding education and race, such the Swann (1985) and Rampton (1981) reports respectively highlighted the need for these issues to be fully addressed. Unfortunately, as with other official reports conducted into race relations in Britain, such as the Lord Scarman enquiries (Scarman, 1981, 1986), lasting recommendations were not comprehensively carried out (Gifford, 1986). It was not until the 1999 Macpherson report into the death of Stephen Lawrence in 1993 that wider social institutions other than the police reflected upon their operations in regard to race, within their bureaucracies, with increased rigour.

On a positive note, not all my sample succumbed to failure within the classroom. Some were able to usefully override these forms of discrimination. Individuals such as Gilly and Pretty were clearly driven to acquire a profitable education and worked diligently and endured hardship in order to achieve this. However, there is an interesting dichotomy between these two individuals and their academic pathways. Pretty, who for the most part was educated in the Caribbean, makes it clear that the culture for success in the Jamaican classroom was potent, and the competitive atmosphere amongst students spurred him on. Having been born in London, but leaving to be educated in Jamaica as a teen, he was quickly made aware of how relevant an education was in a more mechanical and simpler society like Jamaica. This forced him to become even more aware of the need to be academically equipped whilst positioned in a more complex, post-industrial Britain. So naturally he took his studies exceptionally seriously.

By contrast, Gilly achieved his academic success by stealth. He confessed to selling drugs as an undergraduate (to both students and staff), and remained an active member of a street gang in college. However, he made sure his grades were first-rate. Mac an Ghaill (1988, 1994) mentions that this type of strategy is sometimes adopted by black students who are fully aware of the importance of education. They are aware that it may provide an escape from the traditional expectations of themselves as black and working class, but simultaneously adopt subtle acts of resistance to mask their educational commitment to onlookers and peers.

Conclusion

> He [the black male] is made to feel inferior in every way. In addition to being told he is dirty and ugly and 'sexually unreliable', he is told by a variety of means that he is intellectually inferior. When he prepares to

leave school, and even before, he is made to realise that he and his 'kind' are only fit for menial jobs.

(Coard, 1971:28)

The relationship between the post-*Windrush* generation and British education has been tempestuous to say the least, but, unlike some of the other areas covered in this book, it is well documented. Refreshingly the literature offered on this matter is often by black educational practitioners and/or educators themselves, which in my view presents a more relatable debate. The post-*Windrush* generation encountered two significant imperatives within the experience of education: racism and racialisation. Both these factors, as we have seen, shape and fortify existing issues of identity and representation. For those who undertook education in the West Indies at an early age, racism was not openly presented. The main aspect of their education was discipline, which was often administered in the same way as in the home. In fact, strict discipline, physical or otherwise, was a constant theme throughout numerous aspects of their lives. The British experience of schooling, however, was vastly different. The issue of race was a permanent fixture. School location, class streaming and teacher/student engagement, in the perception of those interviewed, was commonly racialised – the stereotypical belief systems surrounding black performance in sport that ran uncontested throughout their schooling experience are a good example. Low expectations of West Indian students were also clearly visible. The teacher mentioned by Blue who suggested the future for black students in his care held in store only 'death or prison' is undoubtedly troubling, but not at all uncommon. According to Coard (1971) and Rist (1977), labelling of this kind is extremely detrimental to the student, as it can stunt personal growth, promote a low self-image, induce anxiety and, in the case of some respondents, act as a self-fulfilling prophecy, and I am sure these so-called professional educators are all too aware of this. Thankfully, however, a counter-narrative can be offered by individuals such as Pretty and Gilly, who, despite the odds, achieved academic excellence. Unfortunately Gilly and Pretty are the exception, rather than the rule (Yekwai, 1988; Christian, 2005).

The idealistic notion held by the *Windrush* arrivals, which suggested that success could only be achieved by a 'good British education', would have been a reasonable conclusion, had the British educational experience been even-handed. Regrettably, the majority of parents, despite holding aspirations for their children, failed to counsel them on how these aspirations could be fulfilled. To be fair, this was perhaps because they did not know how to, and were also oblivious of the severity and harshness that their children faced in British schools.

My dad worked at Ford's on a production line, but wanted me to be a doctor. He never gave me a clue, or went out of his way to find out what I had to do to become a doctor, it was just something he wanted me to do. When I told my teacher I wanted to be a doctor when I grow up, she laughed at me – what chance did I ever have?

(Blue)

References

Althusser, L. (1971) *Lenin and Philosophy and Other Essays*, London: New Left Books.

Back, L., Crabbe, T. & Solomos, J. (2001) *The Changing Face of Football: Racism, Identity and Multiculture in the English Game*, London: Berg Publishers.

Bourdieu, P. (1984) *Distinction: A Social Critique of the Judgement of Taste*, London: Routledge.

Bourdieu, P. (1988) *Homo Academicus*, Stanford: Stanford University Press.

Bowles, S. & Gintis, H. (1976) *Schooling in Capitalist America*, London: Routledge & Kegan Paul.

Christian, M. (2005) 'The Politics of Black Presence in Britain and Black Male Exclusion in the British Education System', *Journal of Black Studies*, 35: 3.

Coard, B. (1971) *How the West Indian Child is Made Educationally Sub-Normal in the British School System: The Scandal of the Black Child in Schools in Britain*, London: Karia Press.

Drew, D. (1995) *'Race', Education and Work: The Statistics of Inequality*, Aldershot: Avebury.

Fanon, F. (1967) *Black Skin, White Masks*, New York: Grove Press.

Garland, J. (2001) *Racism and Anti Racism in Football*, London: Palgrave.

Gifford, L. (1986) *The Broadwater Farm Inquiry*, London: Karia Press.

Gillborn, D. (1995) *Racism and Antiracism in Real Schools*, Buckingham: Open University Press.

Isaac, B. (2001) *The Invention of Racism in Classical Antiquity*, Princeton: Princeton University Press.

King, C. (2000) *Play the White Man: The Theatre of Racialised Performance in the Institutions of Soccer*, London: Goldsmiths College, University of London.

Mac an Ghaill, M. (1988) *Young, Gifted and Black*, Milton Keynes: Open University Press.

Mac an Ghaill, M. (1994) *The Making of Men*, Buckingham: Open University Press.

Monrose, K. (2017) 'Shame, Scandal and Respectability amongst the Children of *Windrush* Generation: A Scholarly Omission', in Hobbs, D. (ed.), *Mischief, Morality and Mobs, Essays in Honour of Geoffrey Pearson*, New York & Abingdon: Routledge, pp. 59–82.

Mullard, C. (1982) 'Multiracial Education in Britain: From Assimilation to Cultural Pluralism', in Tierney, J. (ed.), *Race, Migration and Schooling*, London: Holt, Rinehart & Winston, pp. 120–133.

Newham Monitoring Project (1991) *Forging a Black Community: Asian and Afro Caribbean Struggles in Newham*, London: NMP/CARF.

Oakley, R. (1968) *New Backgrounds: The Immigrant Child at Home and at School*, London: Oxford University Press.

Preston, J. (2007) *Whiteness and Class in Education*, Dordrecht: Springer.

Pryce, K. (1979) *Endless Pressure*, Bristol: Bristol Classical Press.

Rampton Report (1981) *West Indian Children in Our Schools: Interim Report of the Committee of Inquiry into the Education of Children from Ethnic Minority Groups*, London: Home Office.

Rist, R. C. (1977) *On Understanding the Processes of Schooling: The Contribution of Labelling Theory*, Oxford: Oxford University Press.

Scarman, L. (1981) *The Scarman Report*, London: Home Office.

Scarman, L. (1986) *The Scarman Report (Revised edn)*, Harmondsworth: Penguin.

Swann Report (1985) *Education for All: Report of the Committee of Enquiry into the Education of Children from Ethnic Minority Groups*, London: HMSO.

Willis, P. (1977) *Learning to Labour*, London: Saxon House.

Yekwai, D. (1988) *British Racism, Malediction & the Afrikan Child*, London: Karnak House.

Chapter 8

Black British religious instruction

Solemn, morose and monotone Masses; '*blue eyed beasts*'; lightning, fire and brimstone; *Assalamu Alaikom*; '*Bun down Babylon*'; fervent glossolia; effusive evangelism; blonde-haired Jesus; '*Sow a seed*'; the faithful and discreet slave; soulful singing and powerful Pocomania performances. All these expressions fused together collectively form the post-*Windrush* generation's experience of religious observance and instruction in Britain.

Classical sociological thought on race and religion

> From the very beginning of the development of sociology, religion was rec-
> ognised to be a social phenomenon of the utmost importance.
>
> (Wilson, 1982:1)

The so-called founding fathers of the discipline, Auguste Comte and Herbert Spencer, viewed sociology as a replacement for theological interpretations of human existence (Mill, 1865). Within the Reformation period, social action was rationalised according to the standpoint of Christendom, or more specifically Catholicism (Comte & Ferre, 1988). Social conduct, municipal duties and social responsibilities were carried out in order to glorify God, obtain favour and purchase salvation (Hobbhouse, 1915). Comte and his contemporaries attempted to move away from what was regarded as 'primitive fetishism' to a more 'sophisticated' and 'rationalised' approach to explain the true nature of human existence. This new science placed emphasis upon impartial detachment, objectivity and neutrality, the ultimate objective being philosophical autonomy and self-governance. This called for the worship of God to be replaced by the worship of man, suggesting that man is the highest essence of man himself.

The topic of religion has caught the attention of a number of celebrated intellectuals whose sphere of activity expands beyond the realms of sociology:

> The explicit and manifest function of religion is to offer men the prospect
> of salvation, and to provide them with appropriate guidance for its

attainment. Obviously just what is taken to constitute salvation differs from one culture and one religion to another.

(Wilson, 1982:27)

Du Bois (1907) considered religion an integral part of the function of black communities in North America and beyond. Herskovits (1941) expanded on this by suggesting that displaced blacks are an overwhelmingly religious people, whose religious beliefs transcend all other forms of social expression. The shared values and group cohesion that adherents enjoy alleviate and heal the social ills experienced. As a result, personalities are moulded, and identities formed, by virtue of the restorative nature of the church.[1]

'Fire 'pon Rome': the import of Rastafari

As we can attest, West Indians came to Britain schooled in high Christian values and a Calvinist-informed work ethic. For some, securing employment was crucial on two fronts. First, as stated, work enabled a higher level of material existence for them and their families, and second, an important factor to keep in mind within this chapter, it enabled them to proudly serve the 'Mother Country' whilst concurrently returning glory to God (Pryce, 1979). However, the impact of religion on the sociopolitical consciousness of blacks in Britain was not as far-reaching as it was in North America.[2] The maturing second generation of blacks, who faced the harshness of life in Britain, did not readily look to North America for inspiration regarding social justice, as has been assumed. Instead they looked to the Caribbean, fuelled mainly by the popularity at the time of reggae music and the teachings of Rastafari that lay at its core.

The message of Rastafari acted as an undiluted and direct response to the racial prejudice and perceived social injustice the post-*Windrush* generation endured, particularly during the 1970s and 1980s (Cashmore, 1979, 1984). As stated elsewhere, blacks who felt the sting of racism, marginalisation and criminalisation retreated into various forms of blackness and forged identities that assisted in the development of personalised coping mechanisms. Rasta proved to be one of the most enduring of these strategies. The Rastafari movement, whose roots lay in the post-colonial regions of the British West Indies, delivered a radical, uncompromising position, through the medium of reggae music. Central to this belief was the message of Africa as the authentic homeland of Diasporised, dislocated and displaced black people (Garvey, 1986; Lewis, 1997).

Rastafari is the revealed livity for our great ancient Afrikan tradition, giving relevant guidance for today and for the future. It is that which I and I live, and express through our culture as loyal Afrikans.

(Ebanks, 1983:18)

Rastafari,[3] a messianic religio-political movement, upholds the belief that Haile Selassie – Negus TarfariMakomen (His Imperial Majesty the first of Ethiopia) – is divinely appointed as the human manifestation of Almighty God. In addition, Rastafari supposes that Selassie's presence heralded a call for black redemption, and repatriation to Africa for globally displaced black people (Ebanks, 1983; Spencer, 1999). Although Rastafari occupies a crucial space in understanding Black British presence, it is often omitted from mainstream black religious commentary and replaced by denominations such as Pentecostalism and Catholicism (Pryce, 1979; Clark, 1994). This is an oddity given that Rastafari rigorously base their beliefs upon the Pentateuch and Hebrew scriptures within the same body of texts that Catholics and Pentecostals profess to follow.

As black self-awareness and consciousness broadened through the popularisation of reggae music at this time, the impressionable and alienated black British youths began to pose questions regarding their cultural identity and heritage:

> It was all about Rasta for us. Peter Tosh, Burning Spear, Big Youth, and Dennis Brown – they gave us a message that we hadn't heard before; it made sense and felt good; it made us reason and read about our position here, and at the same time healed us from the oppression on the street.
>
> (Fire)

An education in black history that did not begin with the slave trade took place via reggae music, and young blacks became aware that the Caribbean was a merely a staging post for displaced Africans. Some began to recognise that by being located in England they were further away from their 'roots' than they first thought:

> We have to realise that the Caribbean is just like how England is – a place we were sent to work. Our real home is Africa. The Caribbean is where we were *carried beyond,* once we left Africa.
>
> (Pretty)

Burglar remarked that, for the post-*Windrush* generation during the 1970s and 1980s, simply the outward appearance of Rastafari – bearded and donning dreadlocks – transmitted a sense of pride and heightened esteem that educed a level of respectfrom peers:[4]

> I was brought around Rasta. They had straight respect from man on road and put the frighteners on the bull [police], because they stood up for their rights and wouldn't put up with any fuckry.
>
> (Burglar)

New religious movements parallel to Rastafari regularly attract new affiliates because the functions they perform are not ingrained within the dominant culture of society. The socially defined imperatives offered by Rasta were welcomed by peers, but, as we will see, not by West Indian elders, who held their adopted lifestyle in contempt. For older 'Christian'-minded West Indians, Rastafari were rumpled, mentally disturbed, social outcasts who, by virtue of being uncombed and ungroomed, were a disgrace not only to their families but to the wider community of West Indians in Britain:

> My granny did tell me say not to come to her yard again true mi tun Rasta and start fi locks up and stop shave.
>
> (Rambo)

The long, uncombed hair and bearded faces of those who embraced Rastafari were vehemently frowned upon and found unacceptable by their elders, who could not fathom why young men would want to wantonly place themselves in a position of disadvantage:

> You have to comb your hair! I don't know why all these young boys neglect themselves and take on that nastiness. When we first came to England you don't see how we dressed decent in our tie and jacket? These Rasta boys are worthless. What English man will give them a job looking like that?
>
> (Joe)

Sound system performers Miss Irie and Tipper Irie convey the feelings of dismay of West Indian parents at the prospect of their daughters courting a Rastaman, which some considered the worst thing a respectable girl from an upstanding family could do:

> *Me no want me daughter to have no Rasta man,*
> [I don't want my daughter to date a Rasta man]
> *Them head top natty and it dutty man,*
> [Their hair is knotted and dirty]
> *Look how the Rasta man dem tan.*
> [Look at his appearance!]
> *All dem good for, is to smoke the Ganja,*
> [Rasta's only purpose is to smoke cannabis]
> *And me no want none of dem come near me daughter.*
> [I don't want one anywhere near my daughter]

Millie, a law graduate of Jamaican parentage, adds:

> My father told me more times than I could count that Rastas were only good for three things in life: to make spliffs, make trouble and to make illegitimate children.
>
> (Millie)

It was not only family members and elders within black communities who had issues with Rasta. Burglar reflects upon his detention in his youth, when there was no consideration or acknowledgment of Rastafari as a legitimate religious lifestyle, resulting in his dreadlocks being unceremoniously shorn off:

> I went to a Borstal at fifteen. One morning the screws came into my cell, held me down and shaved my hair off. Something changed in me until today towards them people, because the way I saw it was that was an attack on my spirituality.
>
> (Burglar)

As popular as Rastafari was for some of the post-*Windrush* generation, not all were inspired by its doctrine. There remained a number who were disenchanted with their position in society, and questioned all forms of religion, including Rasta. Soldier questioned why there was no black concept of God within his religious upbringing, akin to the teachings of political leader Marcus Garvey:[5]

> Every race seems to have made God to suit their own race, every race apart from black people. Where's the black idea of God? Marcus Garvey, who Rasta's [sic] say is the Black Moses, addressed it to a point, but he was a Roman Catholic, he wasn't a Rasta himself. Same with Haile Selassie. I've seen pictures of him, and he doesn't have locks on his head either.
>
> (Soldier)

Similarly Blue, who was raised in the Catholic Church, questioned some of the key concepts of Catholicism. Here he speaks of the weekly Communion Mass that he was forced to partake in by his parents, as a child:

> To me it [The Eucharist] symbolises cannibalism, eating the body of Christ and drinking his blood! I was thinking hang on a minute, that's not right, but I couldn't question it openly, I just had to accept it. Getting older and understanding the Bible, I know that Communion is not a thing to do every week. Trust me, Ken, the Bible is the only book people buy and don't read.
>
> (Blue)

'Fools go to church on Sunday': religious propriety

> I had to go to church every Sunday whether I liked to or not. That was the regime in our house and that went for everybody. That's how it was, whether you believed or not.
>
> (Gilly)

Religiosity and church attendance are undoubtedly tied to notions of respectability, and gave a visible status to those who were unseen in the white world (Pryce, 1979; Monrose, 2017). Within church, domestic workers were transformed into Sunday school teachers, and bus drivers into pastors. Those who occupied low-status employment outside the church, within it gained prominence and position. For some, this was reason enough to be a member, as a good standing in the church was considered an efficient template for future success in life; as Herberg (1956) suggests, church attendance was perhaps not intrinsically linked to one faith as such, but had more to do with aspiration, community and social obligation.

Although the majority of the cohort no longer regard themselves as churchgoers *per se*, they clearly understood the reasons why their parents encouraged religious attendance. Greenie states:

> It was something that was decided for me. 'You *are* going to church.' So I went to Sunday school and church on a regular basis. It was something forced on me to do because it was supposed to be good for me like medicine, and of course my mum wanted the best for me.
>
> (Greenie)

Nev, whose father is an elder Jehovah's Witness, states that although he is no longer a direct member of the congregation, he still attempts to live his life in accordance with the manner in which he was brought up, and one day sees himself returning to the Kingdom Hall:[6]

> Religion played a big part [in my life]. It never really did me any harm. I still believe that being involved in religion is good. That means there's a chance that I will go back to what I know and become a Witness again one day.
>
> (Nev)

Despite religious instruction being a mandatory rite of passage for the post-*Windrush* generation, the extent and depth of it varied. Some were acolytes (Mr Gold) or choir boys (Fat Larry); some were fully fledged Rastafari (Blue), or Jehovah's Witnesses (Nev). Moreover it is instructive to keep in mind that for black youth during the 1970s and 1980s it was difficult to avoid involvement with the church, as many recreational spaces available to them were youth clubs and other social outlets organised by religious groups:

> We used to go to place called Friday club at Bignold Hall in Forest Gate and play pool, football and music. It was an important place for us because we didn't have anywhere else to go. The catch was that you had to stay on for the religious part of it at the end, but it was worth it still.
>
> (Blue)

Whereas white working-class youth of the same age might have participated in the army cadets or Cub Scouts, black youth, particularly those located within densely populated urban areas like Newham, relied heavily upon the church for extracurricular activities. Parents were of course happy with this, as it reinforced their conviction that involvement with the church aided personal development, and more importantly kept them from trouble on the street. Miss Marie, a retired mother of four, points out that the reasoning behind encouraging her children's participation in the church is one solely based on biblical principles. She states:

> It's written in the Bible that for us to bring up a child in the right way, they have to get to know God, and that means going to church and reading the Bible, and to pray.
>
> (Miss Marie)

Conclusion

Historically, religion has played an integral role in the lives of black people, regardless of their situation or location. In the terms of the post-*Windrush* generation, religious instruction has been a pathway trod by many. Despite its problematic history connected to slavery and colonialism, religious participation has been a functional support mechanism for displaced black people. Within the context of life in the West Indies it provided social bonding, rites of passage and communal solidarity; whilst within the context of Britain's black communities it acted as a social stabiliser for economic migrants, and eased the psychological resentment of alienation, racism and discrimination. Furthermore, religious participation carried with it notions of respectability and propriety. My data shows that religious instruction was instilled in the post-*Windrush* generation at an early age. Nonetheless it became clear that as social consciousness grew, and ideas surrounding self-concept in respect to their newly acquired political status surfaced, the faith of their parents was questioned. Reggae music, intertwined with the doctrine of Rastafari, seemed to address these lingering enquiries squarely, as well as acting as a repository of knowledge of self and black history, which both empowered and informed. Reggae and Rasta provided answers to their social condition that parents, priests, pastors and preachers could not.

Despite religion occupying a central role in the lives of these men whilst growing up, by adulthood its potency weakened. This was not due to a lack of spirituality on their part; on the contrary, maturity has helped many of them solidify their faith. The key difference now is that church attendance and religious ritual are no longer obligatory. Furthermore, although religion perhaps still lies at the core of some black British communities, particularly outside London, it too has succumbed to the process of secularisation to which the wider society has also been subject. As society is increasingly observed in empirical and scientific terms, the importance of religion has waned, and we see modernity typified by a reduction in open religious involvement. An interesting question for further investigation could be: has diminished church attendance, particularly amongst the post-*Windrush* generation, had a negative or positive impact on black communities in Britain? This is a pertinent question, particularly in reference to the following chapter, which is concerned with the ever debatable topic of crime.

Notes

1 I use the term 'church' here loosely, but it is inclusive of the myriad places of worship that members of black communities may attend, for example Mosque, Temple, Kingdom Hall, etc.
2 The American Civil Rights movement allows us to examine the empowerment that religion granted black people in various areas of social life. It is well known that black figures at the helm of the American civil rights movement were strongly linked to religious denominations (Michael 'Martin' Luther King, El Hajj Malik El- Shabazz [Malcolm X] and Adam Clayton Powell Jnr are cases in point). It is also instructive to note that the aforementioned were strongly influenced by the most recognised Jamaican (Usain Bolt and Bob Marley aside), Marcus Garvey, who is often regarded as the forefather of Pan-Africanism. Black institutions of worship allowed for the re-establishment and fortification of the black family unit, particularly in the post-Civil War era of American history, and the rekindling of family ties after the Second World War in Britain (Scanzoni, 1971).
3 There is much debate amongst the houses of Rastafari as to whether Selassie is God in the personality of a man or not. However, the point all Rastas agree upon is that Haile Selassie's presence is in accord with Biblical scripture (explicitly from the lineage of Kings David and Solomon), and he acts as the redeemer of displaced blacks. An investigation of the views held by Rastas within the Jamaican classical period of 1930–60 reveals evidence of a formal decree that was passed, allowing Rastas to be killed on sight. Even an affiliate or sympathiser of Rastafari ran the risk of imprisonment (Ebanks, 1983; Nettleford, 1999). Leonard P. Howell, along with Archibald Dunkley, Joseph Hibbert, Alexander Bedward and Robert Hinds was one of the forefathers who brought Rastafari to Jamaica. He established a headquarters for his Rasta brethren in the Warika Hills, West Kingston, which became known as 'Pinnacle' – essentially a rustic camp where the Rastas lived. Due to extensive police raids, and the eventual incarnation of Howell, the Rasta's were forced to retreat into barren rural parts of Jamaica. What seems to be omitted from the historical account of Rastafari is the unprecedented influence that Eastern religions had upon shaping its system of belief and practices. Indentured East Indian labourers arrived in Jamaica around 1845. This brought with it the presence of classical Hinduism as a major religious force throughout some Caribbean islands, particularly Trinidad and Jamaica. Howell, Hinds, Archibald and Dunkley established a close association with East Indians, and fused the mystical-order beliefs of classical Hinduism with the redemption-seeking model of Garveyism. The dreadlocked, marijuana-smoking Saddhu or 'wandering ascetic' is a well-known figure in India. Bands of Saddhus also often live in Rasta-style camps and smoke marijuana from a formally blessed communal

chalice-pipe, which perhaps acted as a hybrid or prototype for Rastafari practice, with the Pentateuch acting as the earthly guiding force.

4 The Rastafari movement within British black communities had its genesis in the 1960s, and is documented as being located within the Notting Hill area of West London (Ebanks, 1983). The emergence of Rastafari in Britain was heralded by the introduction of the Universal Black Improvement Organisation (UBIO), based on Marcus Garvey's Universal Negro Improvement Association (UNIA), adopting its philosophy of 'One God, One aim, One destiny'.

5 This is an extension of the discourse of Marcus Garvey who encouraged black people to look at God through their own eyes, rather than those of the European (Garvey, 1986; Grant, 2008).

6 Place of worship for Jehovah's Witnesses.

References

Cashmore, E. (1979) *Rastaman: The Rastafarian Movement in England*, London: Unwin.

Cashmore, E. (1984) *The Rastafarians*, London: Minority Rights Group.

Clark, P. (1994) *Black Paradise: The Rastafarian Movement*, San Bernadino: Borgo Press.

Comte, A. & Ferre, F. (1988) *An Introduction to Positive Philosophy*, Indianapolis: Hackett Publishing Company.

Du Bois, W. E. B. (1907) *The World and Africa: An Inquiry into the Part Which Africa Has Played in World History*, New York: The Viking Press.

Ebanks, K. A. (1983) *Rastafari Livity; A Basic Information Text*, London: Kwemara Publications.

Garvey, M. (1986) *Philosophy and Opinions of Marcus Garvey*, Dover: Majority Press.

Grant, C. (2008) *Negro with a Hat: The Rise and Fall of Marcus Garvey*, London: Vintage.

Herberg, W. (1956) *Protestant, Catholic, Jew*, New York: Doubleday.

Herskovits, M. J. (1941) *The Myth of The Negro Past*, New York: Harper & Row.

Hobbhouse, L. T. (1915) *Morals in Evolution; a Study in Comparative Ethics*, New York: Chapman Hill.

Holy Bible King James Version (1611).

Irie, T. & Irie, M. (1989) Sound tape recorded live in Birmingham on Saxon Studio Sound System, personal cassette.

Lewis, W. (1997) *Soul Rebels: The Rastafari*, Long Grove: Waveland Press.

Mill, J. S. (1865) *Auguste Comte and Positivism*, Ann Arbor: University of Michigan Press.

Nettleford, R. (1999) 'Discourse on Rastafarian Reality', in Nathaniel, M., Spencer, W. & McFarlane, A. (eds), *Chanting Down Babylon: The Rastafari Reader*, Kingston: Ian Randle Publishers, pp. 311–326.

Pryce, K. (1979) *Endless Pressure*, Bristol: Bristol Classical Press.

Scanzoni, J. (1971) *The Black Family in Modern Society*, Chicago: Allyn & Bacon.

Spencer, W. (1999) *Dread Jesus*, London: Society for Promoting Christian Knowledge.

Wilson, B. (1982) *Religion in Sociological Perspective*, New York: Oxford University Press.

Chapter 9

Criminal participation, desistance and preclusion

The aim of this chapter is not to investigate whether black men are more pre-disposed to criminality than other racial classifications, but to consider the motivations involved in criminal and non-criminal participation. The narratives offered by Pretty and Blacker are an ideal starting point:

> I didn't want to embarrass myself or my friends and family. I wanted be like one of those positive images of blackness. I didn't want to be a criminal statistic. If you were involved in crime any sort of crime at all. I stayed well away from you.
>
> (Pretty)

From an early age, Pretty made a conscious decision to avoid criminal activity at any cost. A criminal pathway, he believed, would hinder his aspirations, and cause embarrassment and humiliation to his family and friends. Despite grow-ing up in a part of East London where a street-tough reputation of being a bad boy was considered an asset, he had no qualms in labelling himself a 'good boy'. Blacker, on the other hand, by virtue of his peer-group association, became well known as a figure of notoriety:

> They [his parents] would say, 'You have too many friends – stop follow-ing your friends them and getting in trouble'. But I wouldn't listen. I was the man on the streets back then. I was a leader. People followed me and wanted to be around me, it wasn't me following them.
>
> (Blacker)

In tandem with issues of peer-group association, loosening of ties within the community, whether through employment, familial estrangement or educational expulsion, can also pressure a drift into crime. The work of Hirschi (1967, 1969) is readily usable and relevant to this area, as it seeks to address not why crime is committed, but why it is *not* committed, which for me is an interest-ing line of interrogation. Hirschi noticed that for some, *shame* acts as a significant factor in the preclusion of criminal activity. Within this context, shame can be defined bilaterally: it can mean to have respect for oneself and one's reputation (pride), or to draw dishonour or disgrace to oneself or one's family and friends, as outlined by Pretty earlier.

Shame and respectability are of crucial importance within West Indian culture, as they act as core methods of social control, and are historically imbedded within the cultural consciousness of the people:

> Being West Indian and being a criminal brings shame and scripture on your family. I can proudly say that being forty-six years old and having left home at seventeen, no policeman had been to my mother's house and said I've been involved in a shoplifting or a shooting. Because of that I can hold my head up high.
>
> (Nev)

> For my dad it was all about the family name. It's stuck in my brain; do not disrespect or shame the family name.
>
> (Fire)

> We grew up over here seeing so many negative images of black people all over the place, and most of it had to do with crime. Our parents didn't want us to fall in that type of bracket. We as youngsters knew that we had to behave ourselves or else we would be labelled a criminal and that would bring down shame on them.
>
> (Pretty)

Shaming strategies within complex industrialised societies have not been fully utilised as an effective method of crime prevention, because they are seen as outdated and wholly reliant upon micro interaction and relaxed prescribed relationships. Moreover, the importance of shaming is considered dependent upon the significance of shame within the cultural group. Small communal settings like the communities in the West Indies are fundamental for it to successfully function:

> It would seem that sanctions imposed by relatives, friends or a personally relevant collective, have more effect on criminal behaviour than sanctions imposed by legal authority.
>
> (Braithwaite, 1989, cited in Muncie, 1999:433)

Two typologies of shaming can be used to discuss the experiences of the post-*Windrush* generation: disintegrative and regenerative. Disintegrative shaming is primarily concerned with the stigmatisation of an individual who is considered beyond redemption, and often labelled an outcast. Regenerative shaming, on the other hand, leaves room for redemption, but only if the application of preventive measures is on the basis of a moral sense of right and wrong can it be truly successful. Scheff et al. (1989) suggest that a central feature within our lives is the search for honour and integrity, which in their view is why shaming ultimately proves to be effective. Carrabine et al. (2004) concur with this by suggesting, 'We want and need the social approval of others' (Carrabine et al., 2004:63). So, what is shaming in the context of the lives of the post-*Windrush* generation? Simply put, it involved the expression of emotional disapproval by the community, peers and kin, in an attempt to invoke remorse. Those who held pronounced criminal pathways, such as Blacker, Blue, Fat Larry, Gilly and Soldier, all mention that at some point they had encountered a crisis of conscience with regard to the shame and the anguish brought upon their respected families as a result of their criminal exploits:

> I was inside looking out. My old man came to visit me [in prison] and was just bawling, I'd never seen him like that, and it made me bawl too. I said, 'I can't make them [his parents] go through this shit any more'. Even when I was involved in those shootings, I lied, and told them it was a stabbing to lessen the blow.
>
> (Blacker)

Criminal pathways

So, what then is the impetus that provoked individuals in this study to drift into crime? Whilst my sample group does not account for the experiences of the entire post-*Windrush* generation in terms of criminality, I deem it representative enough to provide a sufficient level of insight into this topic. As we know, one of the most commonly fixed themes within sociological discourse on race in Britain surrounds the criminalisation of black men and black culture, and the ensuing relationship between them and the criminal justice system.

Despite the overwhelming number of black men who reject criminal pathways and operate their lives within the parameters of the law, officially presented statistics still show an over-representation of black men within the various branches of the criminal justice system, which gives the impression that black men are more prone to committing crime than any other racial group. Reasons for offending are complex and are subject to motivation and context. However, the data unearthed in this project suggests that the underlying motivation for embarking on a criminal pathway lies in the matter of social exclusion, because, as I have established, an individual who perceives that they are excluded from the social order is more likely to manifest disaffection (Merton, 1938; Agnew & Passas, 1997; Young, 1999). Blacker provides us with an account of what social exclusion looked like under Thatcherism for young black men in Newham during the 1980s.

Being expelled from the formal educational system at the age of fourteen resulted in Blacker spending most of his time loitering on the streets. Inevitably, he made acquaintances among those in a similar position as himself. He idled time away in amusement arcades, drug dens or simply on road. Blacker believed his drift into crime at the age of fourteen was inescapable, as he was excluded from school eleven times before eventually being expelled permanently. What made matters worse was that governance in Newham refused to afford him an alternative method of schooling, which patently arrested his educational development. The educational system, he believes, regarded him as a lost cause, and beyond redemption:

> So that period is when it really went wrong. I was interviewed at nearly every school in Newham, but got rejected. Nobody wanted to take me in. I guess being excluded so many times made me too bad to handle, so I was just forgotten about.
>
> (Blacker)

Expulsion impinged on his self-confidence, self-esteem and self-respect, and as a result he saw crime as a means of escape and coping strategy:

> After all those rejections that's when I really hit it [crime]. I was full time. It was something that I just felt I had to do. I was coming out my yard [house], and roaming the streets looking for something to commit.
>
> (Blacker)

Crime acted as an outlet for his frustrations and feelings of injustice at this pivotal point of his life. However, more importantly, and in response to established theoretical considerations, he believed crime allowed him to regain and replenish the lost respect he had experienced. Therefore, although his educational development was stunted, his street-level respect and street-corner capital soared, and having respect on the street was all that mattered to those subject to broader socio-economic and politically imposed restraints:

> I lost the plot and I didn't care. When I got kicked out [of school] I really started hitting crime hard. Society didn't care about me, so fuck it, I didn't care about society. I made easy money, money to squander. I couldn't take the money home and say to my mum, 'There you go, mum, here's a score', I had to spend it. So I would buy a draw of weed, go arcade, and feast on fast food. It was good living at the time, and the thing was I had respect from people around me, because I always had something going on, and always a bit of money on me.
>
> (Blacker)

Quickly, he found out how easy it was to make money this way. As well as hitting back at society, one of his main objectives was to 'live good' and enjoy access to easy money. This had the dividend of being held in high esteem by his peer group, by being known as 'an earner' and competent 'hustler', which were paramount prerequisites for 'respect' within many marginalised communities in Newham during this time (Hobbs, 1988). Once gained, respect was augmented by moving away from petty and opportunist crime towards burglary and distribution of illegal drugs (a topic that will be explored later in the chapter).

Now he is aware that this period of his life was valuable, and had he been in school, his life might well have developed differently. His voice is tinged with regret whilst he recollects what he considers the 'lost years' of his youth:

> Those were priceless years. If I was in school it could have changed the course of my life.
>
> (Blacker)

Blue, like Blacker, is another individual who turned to crime after feeling the sting of social exclusion. Due to a racially motivated infraction at work, Blue had the unfortunate experience of losing the job he had held since leaving school and becoming an apprentice. Blue still rues this experience, as it was a job he loved and had aspired to:

Monrose: So what happened when you left school?
Blue: I got a job as YTS [youth training scheme] apprentice on the council, but as I got older I noticed different things at work.
Monrose: Such as?
Blue: Well the racism and things like that that happened in your face. People making jokes about your colour and the way you look.

Blue confessed that whilst growing up in Newham during the 1980s, so prevalent and open was the racism that he thought hatred of black people was 'just how life was'. He recalled regularly seeing racist graffiti such as YNF (Young National Front), NF (National Front) and, BM (British Movement) liberally daubed around the housing estate where he lived, and no effort was made by Newham council to eradicate it, and was simply considered part of the natural surroundings:

> I had a big NF symbol drawn on the wall of my house – it was there for years. It didn't even register after a while. It was everywhere else as well, so being on my front wall didn't really matter.
>
> (Blue)

As he matured, he became aware of the extent and toxicity of the racism that surrounded him.

> Travelling from Forest Gate, and going to other parts of the area like Canning Town and East Ham, I really saw how racist Newham was and how much people hated blacks.
>
> (Blue)

Subsequent unemployment prompted Blue to remove himself from what he considered 'the white man's society' and choose to embrace the lifestyle of Rastafari. What followed was not only an increased distrust of authority but a rebellion against many of society's established rules, which he no longer saw as valid to his existence:

> I was just fed up of having to deal with the white man and his laws. I was out of work and looking a place to live, but nothing was happening, so I did a move and found a squat. I had to eat so I started shotting [selling drugs]. I was making good money too.
>
> (Blue)

Blue saw society's expectation of securing employment and accommodation as an additional burden to the perceived level of racism he felt through everyday interactions. To deal with these difficulties, he turned to illicit activity, and he remains totally unrepentant as he believes he was forced to resort to illegal activity in order to subsist:

> I had to survive. I tried to do it the right way, but the Babylon [police/government/capitalism] wouldn't let me, so I had to find my own way. Besides it's not like I'm selling stuff I wouldn't take. It's not like it was coke or crack, just some brain food.
>
> (Blue)

In Fat Larry's case, domestic violence seemed to be the spur for his drift into crime. As outlined previously, Fat Larry was subjected to unremitting physical violence in the home. Added to this was the saturation of violence around him on the streets of Newham, which even seeped into his school:

> At school if the teacher said something to you that you didn't like, you'd do him, and if he stood [fought back], then five or six of us would jump him, and lay into him. We used to love fighting other schools too. We had a teacher in the woodwork department we'd get tools off. He'd say, 'Make sure you bring them back clean, boys'. We'd go to Lakehouse, Forest Gate and Woodside to fight – that's what school

was all about for me – fighting, being lawless, taking liberties with people, you know, taking advantage.

(Fat Larry)

No surprise that episodes such as these had the inevitable consequence of moulding him into a figure that was readily prone to violence as he matured:

I went to school first year, second year and third year – that was it really. After that I was just on the street. When I was in school I spent most of the time outside the headmaster's office – I was the school bully. I would beat people up and nick their money, but it wasn't my fault. All I had learnt from home and on the street was how to be violent. My parents made me into a really mad and angry person, so looking back I think I took it out on other people. Whatever I wanted I took, and if you crossed me you'd suffer, simple as that.

(Fat Larry)

This persona followed Fat Larry into adulthood, where he felt pressured to constantly prove himself to his peers by continually demonstrating his proficiency in physical violence:

I walked out of school and just carried on being violent; I wanted to be the 'baddest' man out there, and would do anything just to prove myself. I'd knock you down if you tried to get in my way.

(Fat Larry)

The urge behind this motivation to be the 'baddest' was to restock street-level respect (Anderson, 1999; Monrose, 2016). Fat Larry made sure he was a 'face' in East London and Essex. He raved (went partying/clubbing) six or seven times a week. He drove expensive cars, wore opulent clothing and donned expensive jewellery. He even boasted of regularly 'buying out the bar' (purchasing drinks for the night for every patron in a nightclub or venue). Excessive social activity such as this required financing, so Fat Larry began to thieve, burgle and rob in order to obtain the funds to maintain his demanding social life, and garner attention.

Some blokes are back seat drivers – you know they're at it, but want to keep a low profile. I wasn't like that. I wanted people to know who I was and what I did. I was a thief and would nick anything I could physically carry. Dipping [pickpocketing], burglaries, robberies, anything, but at the same time I was still raving. So as quick as the money was coming in, was as quick as it went out again. Thieving and hustling became my full-time job, and I had built up a good reputation as a fence and a thief all over the country.

(Fat Larry)

Theft led to more serious incidents such as a series of armed robberies, which yielded Fat Larry and his associates a great deal of money:

> We used to check this bloke in North London who we'd get our sawn-offs from on a pay-as-you-go type of thing. He was well respected and became a very good mate of mine in the end. We made a lot of money together.
>
> (Fat Larry)

Securing street-level respect from peers is one the most significant themes in the discourse related to the commencement of criminal behaviour. Through the quest for street status and respect, personas are transformed in order to better position deviant and violent behaviour. It is as if a new subgroup develops within an already existing subculture. This distinguishes itself by shunning mainstream norms and values, and maintains itself by the creation of its own personal values, and the construction of alternative standards of conduct.

Desistance and cessation of criminal activity

The following line of investigation is concerned with the desistance and cessation of crime. This again is a significant area for inspection as it is an obvious lacuna in criminological scholarship, particularly in reference to race, and may perhaps offer an insight on why the overwhelming number of black men in Britain refuse and rebuff a criminal pathway.

For Blacker, the reason for stopping crime was simple – parenthood. Becoming a father and husband at a relatively young age induced what he describes as a 'spiritual awakening':

> What stopped crime for me more than anything else was the birth of my child. When my wife was pregnant I was touched by what I can only describe as a spiritual force that just changed me. I felt the baby inside my wife's stomach and just thought, 'Wow, this is me. Someone who is entirely reliant on me'. I felt a bond straight away. I said, 'I'm not going back to jail again'. Before I was prepared to do a bird [serve a prison sentence] for a raise. Now I'm not prepared to go back to jail and walk away from my daughter.
>
> (Blacker)

Like Blacker, Fat Larry describes the pivotal moment that prompted him to stop committing crime:

> I was doing a blag [an armed robbery] in a post office, and I got trapped in the building. I had a carpet [£300] in one hand, and a shotgun in the other, but knew the police were on their way because the fucking alarm was going off. I don't know how I did it, but I managed to get out without

being caught. That was the closest I've been to getting pinched. I suddenly realised what the turn out of doing bird would be. At the time Maggie [Thatcher] was handing out big bird, and loads of people around me were getting a ten or fifteen for crap. I didn't want to be away from my family in that way, so I stopped – simple as that.

(Fat Larry)

Here again we notice the significance of formal bonds. Fat Larry and Blacker saw a prison sentence as an obstacle to their position as fathers and husbands, and were troubled that these roles would be compromised by the harsher penal sentencing structures that were being imposed by the government. For them prison meant isolation from loved ones, and the inevitable outpouring of shame and humiliation. It is as though these factors failed to pique them until they were responsible for a family of their own. Those who, up until the point of parenthood, had relied upon criminal activity as an established part of their lives underwent a transformation in their behaviour when faced with the prospect of losing the respect of those closest to them. Before becoming a father, the adopted adage 'he who has nothing has nothing to lose' resonated strongly. However, fatherhood and marriage meant that street life was scrutinised and the potential outcome of actions taken seriously. Blacker, for example, was victim of a shooting that highlighted his mortality. Thoughts of retribution haunted him for an extended period, before he realised the long-term encumbrance and impediment such a reprisal would cause:

Being shot whilst my wife was pregnant gave me a whole new perspective on things, and made me look at myself and what I was doing in a different way. I had to make a change, and make some difficult decisions.

(Blacker)

'One hot Guinness stout and a stick of sensi': the influence of drugs and alcohol

The subject of drugs and alcohol has a common place within debates on crime, and we often see the two issues paraded in tandem (South, 1998; Tierney & Hobbs, 2003; Fraser & Moore, 2011). Alcohol use seemed not as prevalent amongst the post-*Windrush* generation as with the *Windrush* arrivals, who were referred to by Fire as 'white rum and betting shop men'. Drug use, however, was openly and candidly spoken about. The men who went on to become heavily involved in crime spoke of dabbling in and experimenting with drugs from an early age. Blacker, for example, freely states: 'I'd often buy a draw of weed or solid [cannabis/hashish]. I started smoking weed proper from all I was ten years old.' For those who used drugs, cannabis was the most popular choice. Why this was the case is open to speculation, but both Burglar and Fire believe it was heavily influenced by the music of the period, which carried various themes of cannabis use:

> We guys would listen to reggae when I was coming up, and reggae was talking about weed. Columbia colly, Chalice in the palace, Pick up the Rockers – those were the tunes we raved to and understood.
>
> (Fire)

> Weed smoking is part of me, and my culture. Cokey [whites] will go to the pub, drink fifteen pints, eat a kebab, go home and piss in the wardrobe. Next day he'd say he had a great night out. We'd rather smoke a spliff [a cannabis cigarette], listen some tune [music], and just chill. That's how a black man flexed back then.
>
> (Burglar)

Arguably, at its zenith, in terms of influence at the time, reggae music had a great impact on the consciousness of blacks in Britain in the 1970s and 1980s. Rebellion, protest, social commentary and black history were typical themes of reggae, fused with the spiritual aspect of Rastafari. The music spoke of 'the herb' (cannabis) as the 'healing of nation', and of its proficiency to provide relief from the exploitative nature of life in 'Babylon'. Consequently, cannabis use within the black communities developed into an individual subcultural identity, which was frequently stigmatised and subject to criminalisation. Of cannabis use Blue and Fire state:

> I guess that's what this Babylonian system would call criminal activity, but under whose jurisdiction are they judging it? They call it crime, I call it my culture. I don't class weed as a drug. If you want drugs go to the doctor and he will give it to you.
>
> (Blue)

> It makes me laugh, when we used burn [smoke cannabis] back in the day, it was a problem, an epidemic. Now years later because white people are burning openly on road, it's OK and acceptable.
>
> (Fire)

As harmless as drugs like cannabis professed to be amongst those who used and distributed it, there were those for whom it acted as a pathway into involvement with so-called hard drugs.

Carrabine et al. (2004) describe the 1980s as a watershed decade in terms of the international drugs trade, notable for the increased availability and commoditisation of drugs such as heroin, cocaine and amphetamine-based agents such as ecstasy.[1] The outcome of these developments touched numerous regions globally, and blighted many communities. The black communities in Britain were no exception, and witnessed the devastating impact of drugs such as crack cocaine (Silverman, 1994). Arguably, crack was one of a number of conduits that led to an emergence of gun culture in black communities, as well as being, for some, an additional underlying cause of weakening physical and mental health. It is with interest that we also notice the development of status groups in respect of drug use within maligned communities. For example, powdered cocaine use fitted the ambitious upwardly mobile and entrepreneurial type of individual, whereas its derivative crack was said to be more commonly used by unsophisticated and dicey members of the community, even though both groups simultaneously occupied similar spaces (Lowinson, 2004).

A soldier's story

Soldier confessed to having experimented with crack cocaine to the point of addiction after graduating from cannabis. Prior to this he enjoyed many years of success as an entrepreneur and promoter within London's nightclub scene. This success saw him flourish financially and enjoy a great deal of street-level respect. However, he found the demands of maintaining this type of lifestyle difficult once crack became part of the landscape:

> I was the life and soul of the party. Everybody knew me. My swagger was up. I had the girls, the houses, the cars, and money *and* the influence – the full belly. I had it all. Trust me, Ken, I was wearing Louis Vuitton and Patek Philippe before road people knew what that was, but the truth is I couldn't handle it. Getting it was easy; keeping it is a different thing. I got roped in with the wrong people with bad habits, and started to slip on my own fat. I never ever thought I would fall as far as I did.
>
> (Soldier)

Now a reformed user, Soldier describes the depths to which he sank due to crack abuse:

> I ended up in South [London] living *in* a crack house. Did you hear what I said, Ken? I wasn't visiting the crack house, I was living there. I sold everything I had, and knocked [stole from] everyone around me. I even stole the sheets and pillow cases from my mum's bed to buy crack. I had no shame man – I just loved to get high. I could easily spend £500 a day on crack, seven days a week. My habit was so bad that the dealers used to fight each other to sell to me because they knew they could bathe off of me [make profit].
>
> (Soldier)

Soldier finally decided to stop using crack when he realised his life had spiralled out of control. He eventually became homeless, penniless and friendless.

This was difficult for him to accept as he was once admired and very well known throughout London's black communities. He became estranged from his long-term fiancée, who in time left him permanently, and was eventually disowned by his family. All that remained were the clothes he stood in, and in his own words, 'my pipe'. Soldier was desperate, and moved from London to look for a new start, believing that being away from 'certain people and things' would help improve his circumstances. Unfortunately, the cycle of drug abuse continued whilst located in another city. However, this time the consequences of his actions were to become much worse. Being a newly arrived outsider in a fresh community, he found it easier to steal, dupe and bilk again, but he discovered that his behaviour involved serious ramifications with members of the criminal underworld. Without being aware of it, Soldier was associating with a number of villainous figures, who were connected to even more iniquitous and sinister individuals:

> There are certain people you just should not mess with – I mean the heavy duty faceless and nameless ones who run things, but fly low. With the crack cocaine in my brain I wasn't thinking straight, and was scamming these people hard. Luckily I woke up one day and realised what I was doing, and just had to leave town.
>
> (Soldier)

Soldier ended up in Scotland, and decided to look for help and seek a lasting solution to his drug addiction. He joined an evangelical church, received baptism and is now a fully committed Christian. He believes that it was God who helped him. 'Ken, I was stripped to the bare bones and it was God who turned my life around'.

Like Soldier, Blacker also explained in detail his experiences with crack cocaine, and makes particular references to the cycle that induced him to try the drug:

> No friend of yours would give you crack! If a friend gives you crack he's not your friend, especially if he smokes it himself, and knows what it does.
>
> (Blacker)

He revealed his first experience of taking crack, with a group of men he associated with:

> I was hanging out with these guys I used to thieve and smoke weed with, then one day someone started smoking that fucking thing in front of me. Next thing I know I'm trying it. That was my first taste. This was the early days of crack in the late 1980s. It was disgusting, horrible – it makes you crave. Imagine the same night we went out to lick off a drum

[burgle a house] to get money to buy more crack. We lick off the drum at nine [o'clock], went back to our place at ten thirty, smoked till midnight, and then out again to lick off another drum straight after that to buy more rocks – pure fucking madness. After two burglaries I was left with a tenner in my pocket – the rest got smoked.

(Blacker)

Blacker considered himself fortunate that he did not become fully immersed in the cycle of crack abuse and crime, because, as he claimed when speaking about his criminal activity, it was the financial gain that motivated him more than anything else to commit. He quickly realised that using crack meant he would face too many disadvantages, loss of money being one of them, and reasoned that dealing crack was better than using it. This is echoed by Gilly, who dealt crack (although he never admitted using the drug). Financial gain was his objective, and he speaks in detail of the profits that he made:

Nothing like crack money, let me tell you, Ken, but remember the chemist is the most important link. If he doesn't know how to chef it, then your profit margin is fucked. Crack has small amount of cocaine in it; the majority of the other ingredients are dirt cheap. A dealer with a good chef can get fat quick. Let's say I get a key [kilo] of coke for thirty bags [£30,000] – you know how many rocks I can get out of that? If I cook a minimum amount of cocaine to make the rock, I can all triple my money. It's a good business if you've got the heart for it.

(Gilly)

Similar to Soldier and Blacker, Gilly regards negative peer-group pressure and ease of availability as key components in becoming involved with crack. By virtue of spending much of his time on the street, Gilly drifted into a gang who were actively involved in the distribution of drugs. However, it was a desire to realise his potential, and a thirst for a good education, that prompted him to desist:

My dad always promoted and pushed education, so I wanted a good education, a good respectable university education. When I was younger I got caught up in road life so that couldn't happen, and anyway that wasn't a real option for black guys, especially West Indians back then; besides my spars [peers] would just laugh at me if they found out. Then one day when I was chatting to my brethren and he was telling me about all the prison time he had done. I looked at him, and thought, 'You know what, you ain't got no fucking prospects in life. There's no future for you other than doing more bird, and that will be me in a few years too, because I'm doing the same stupid shit as you.' That was it, I had to fix up. So

I applied to do a degree in business and economics. I did the degree, went on to do a MBA. Now I work for a blue-chip company.

(Gilly)

Gilly's testimony adds an additional twist to an already complex topic. Although his criminality was carried out in order to impress and gain the respect of the gang, in time he realised that the respect he sought would inevitably lead to his own destruction by means of a lengthy prison sentence. This would crush his dream of obtaining an education, and the authentic type of formal respect he craved – respect in the eyes of mainstream society.

By way of these examples, we can see that a search for respect for some is not only responsible for drawing them towards crime but, more importantly, also responsible for repelling them from it.

Conclusion

This chapter has highlighted a number of factors that neutralise 'good boys' away from crime, and magnetise 'bad boys' toward it. First we are able to comprehend that the inclination to drift into crime of some members of the post-*Windrush* generation was a response to wider social contexts, such as school expulsion, unemployment and domestic violence, as well as issues related to peer-group association, and prompted by systematic inequalities of race and class rooted at the core of British society. Not for a moment am I suggesting that criminal acts be excused or absolved; that would be improper. What I am saying is that existing reflections on race and crime require a greater consideration of context, in order to recognise the potential destructive outcomes that discrimination within core institutions, such as those in education and employment, can cause in a longitudinal sense. Nonetheless, however relatable the arguments may be for social ills spurring criminality, they do not stand alone; the criminalisation of black men by enforcement agencies, too, should not be ignored. It is also interesting to note that issues such as respect, which often encourage criminality, also prompted desistance and the cessation of criminal activity.

One of the many original contributions that this ethnography has made to sociological scholarship in reference to race in Britain is that criminal preclusion was a central feature in the lives of the post-*Windrush* generation. Traditionally, this was firmly established in the home, by notions of respectability and shame, and as we have seen, this strategy was very successful in curtailing any potential for a criminal drift. However, in the opinion of some respondents, the potency of shaming has lessened, as West Indians have discarded their own cultural principles in favour of Britishness, particularly in regards to community cohesion and familial configuration. For some, this speaks to the current woes surrounding weapon-enabled crime and so-called gang violence:

> Crime prevention begins at home. I didn't commit crime because the shame it would bring down would be worse than any prison sentence, and being from a tight West Indian family, I'd catch hell. Nowadays though those solid West Indian values have gone, and these youngsters don't have the same level of shame we did. It's like the more money and status we get, this less we look out for each other, and the more diluted our culture becomes.

(Pretty)

Note

1 MDMA, or Methylenedioxymethamphetamine.

References

Agnew, R. & Passas, N. (1997) 'The Nature and Determinants of Strain: Another Look at Durkheim and Merton', in Agnew, R. & Passas, N. (eds), *The Future of Anomie Theory*, Boston: Northeastern University Press, pp. 27–51.
Anderson, E. (1999) *Code of the Streets: Decency, Violence and the Moral Life of the Inner City*, New York: Norton.
Braithwaite, J. (1989) *Crime, Shame and Reintegration*, Cambridge: Cambridge University Press.
Carrabine, E., Lee, M., Plummer, K., South, N. & Iganski, P. (2004) *Criminology: A Sociological Introduction*, London: Routledge.
Fraser, S. & Moore, D. (2011) *The Drug Effect: Health, Crime & Society*, New York: Cambridge University Press.
Hirschi, T. (1967) *Delinquency Research*, New York: Free Press.
Hirschi, T. (1969) *Causes of Delinquency*, Berkeley: University of California Press.
Hobbs, D. (1988) *Doing the Business*, Oxford: Oxford University Press.
Lowinson, J. (2004) *Substance Abuse: A Comprehensive Textbook*, Philadelphia: Lippincott Williams & Wilkins.
Merton, R. K. (1938) 'Social Structure and Anomie', *American Sociological Review*, 3 (5): 672–682.
Monrose, K. (2016) 'Struggling, Juggling and Street Corner Hustling: The Street Economy of Newham's Black Community', in Antonopoulos, G. (ed.), *Illegal Entrepreneurship, Organized Crime and Social Control, Essays in Honor of Professor Dick Hobbs*, Geneva: Springer, pp. 73–84.
Muncie, J. (1999) *Youth & Crime*, London: Sage.
Scheff, T. J., Retzinger, S. M. & Ryan, M. T. (1989) 'Crime, Violence and Self Esteem: Review and Proposals', in Mecca, A., Smelser, N. J.& Vasconcellos, J. (eds), *The Social Importance of Self-Esteem*, Berkeley: University of California Press, pp. 165–199.
Silverman, J. (1994) *Crack of Doom*, London: Headline.

South, N. (1998) *Drugs: Cultures, Control and Everyday Life*, Thousand Oaks & London: Sage.

Tierney, J. & Hobbs, D. (2003) 'Alcohol Related Crime and Disorder Data: Guidance for Local Partnerships', *Home Office Online Research Report*, 1–28.

Young, J. (1999) *The Exclusive Society: Social Exclusion, Crime and Difference in Late Modernity*, Thousand Oaks & London: Sage.

Chapter 10

Conclusion

Whilst the study does not lay claim to represent the entire population of the post-*Windrush* generation of men, for which further study is needed, many of the narratives that are harnessed within this text act as a usable resource for understanding the multiplicity of interpretations surrounding the intersectionality of race, class and gender in modern British society. In order to address my initial aims and objectives, this project at times leant upon some of the key expressions of critical race theory, such as counter storytelling and narrative usage, to offer an alternative research methodology to assist in rearticulating and reframing the idea of race in Britain. Through this method, it emerges that social exclusion and discrimination are often reinforced by an overlapping of existing social constructions related not only to race but applicable also to class and gender, in ways that are unique and distinct to Britain.

The historical impact of difference, whether on the basis of race, social position or gender, grounded within the philosophical reasoning of the Enlightenment period, is very evident today. This has led to a precarious and marginal existence for some, and has prompted a need to utilise an alternative means of societal interaction in order to acquire a viable footing within the social order. Therefore, it is here that we see issues form around self-concept and identities, and the veils and masks mentioned by Du Bois and Fanon. The same is true for masculine hegemony where we see the black male constricted to the periphery of society, and compelled to adopt the habitus imbedded within European concepts of masculinity. Although at times troublesome, this has the benefit of endowing the black male with a unique standpoint, since in addition to being acquainted with the nuanced nature of his own cultural modality, he also gains an understanding and acute awareness of the procedures that dictate the operations of the majority group. Hence we can gain a better appreciation of the comments offered by individuals like Chester the cabbie in the opening chapter:

> Listen, young man, if you're smart in this country, you can be anybody you want to be, at any time. You can be an African, West Indian or an Englishman. Being a black man in this country is easy, you just have to know what part to play.

As well as noticing how just embedded racism has been within British society both before and after the arrival of *Windrush,* this ethnography identifies how ordinary and common is its manifestation within daily interactions and both institutional and occupational cultures, proving recent statements from varying parts of the political spectrum suggesting Britain is now a post-racial society to be erroneous. This can be easily validated by examining the voting patterns of the British electorate during the UK European Union membership referendum of 2016, where we see the issue of immigration – read race – develop as a specific focus of attention.

Very few areas within recent sociological investigation exist where established typologies of black life in Britain have been successfully challenged to a lasting degree. Primary institutions within society have historically mandated the delineation of blacks without agency and consultation. This necessitates that black people in Britain *must* define themselves, for themselves, and mandate their own narratives, instead of resigning, and allowing others, with only a superficial acquaintance of their passage, to do so. For example, during the 1950s and 1960s blacks in Britain were defined as 'coloureds', in the 1970s they were West Indians, through the 1980s and 1990s they were Afro Caribbean, and now, well into this millennium, they are defined as 'black British' – but never English.

Currently blackness, or the black aesthetic, is referred to as 'urban', a myopic and loaded linguistic code that conjures negative imagery of decay and disaffection. Nonetheless, whilst one can quite easily attest to the multitude of inequalities in British society, scholarly balance also notes some of the advances made in Britain in terms of recalibrating her stance on racial difference. The data presented within this ethnography demonstrates that not all members of the post-*Windrush* generation feel compelled to refer to the West Indies as 'home', which during the 1970s and 1980s was practically unheard of. This can clearly be seen in the debate surrounding the recent *Windrush* scandal, where we witness the collective mobilisation of blacks of West Indian descent to hold fast to the right to be acknowledged and treated as British citizens. The outpourings from the Hostile Environment Policy in reference to the post-*Windrush* generation have transformed the mysterious and ambiguous nature of Britishness for black people. In what is undeniably a significant political moment, we see Britishness shift from a concept tied to race into a concept that is intrinsically tied to civil duty, allegiance and presence, which in itself is not far removed from the stance of the 1948 *Windrush* arrivals, who, let us not forget or be misguided, were extremely patriotic.

Incompleteness is an inevitable part of any ethnographic process, and we must keep in mind that our present continually becomes part of our past. I am not claiming to have discussed all the issues facing black men in Britain – space could not allow for this. However, my initial objective of presenting a portrait of the lives of the post-*Windrush* generation is a goal I believe has been suitably accomplished.

The last word belongs to Fire:

I am British. I like fish and chips. I like pie and mash with liquor. Of course I like rice and peas, yellow yam, breadfruit, and all that good stuff, but I'm still British and why not? When I get off the plane at Gatwick, I'm glad to be here. I'm glad to be home. Yeah, it's nice to visit St Kitts, America or whatever, but this is my home, my gaff, my ends, and my manor, and I'm here to stay.

(Fire)

Index